AN I·N·D·I·A·N
in White America

Mark Monroe

EDITED BY Carolyn Reyer

AFTERWORD BY Kenneth Lincoln

AN I·N·D·I·A·N
in White America

TEMPLE UNIVERSITY PRESS

PHILADELPHIA

Temple University Press, Philadelphia 19122
Copyright © 1994 by Temple University. All rights reserved
Published 1994
Printed in the United States of America

The paper used in this publication meets the minimum requirements of
American National Standard for Information Sciences—Permanence of
Paper for Printed Library Materials, ANSI Z39.48-1984 ⊗

Library of Congress Cataloging-in-Publication Data

Monroe, Mark, 1930–
    An Indian in White America / Mark Monroe ; edited by Carolyn Reyer ;
afterword by Kenneth Lincoln.
        p. cm.
    ISBN 1-56639-234-9 (alk. paper). — ISBN 1-56639-235-7 (pbk. :
alk. paper)
    1. Monroe, Mark, 1930– . 2. Oglala Indians—Biography.
I. Reyer, Carolyn, 1919– . II. Title.
E99.O3M666 1994
978.3′004975—dc20
[B]   94-2065

IN MEMORY OF   Emma Monroe

Terry Monroe, Sr.

Amy (Kandi) Monroe

Jenny and Felix Lone Wolf

Minnie and Bill Monroe

and

Mary Anne Monroe Gasser

C•O•N•T•E•N•T•S

E·D·I·T·O·R'S P·R·E·F·F·A·C·E

I first became interested in Mark Monroe's work after reading an article he wrote for the 1982 Presbyterian Church (USA) Mission Yearbook of Prayer describing how he started a nutrition program for Indians and other minority people with the support of the Presbyterian Hunger Fund. I was most impressed by Mark's words and wrote to him. He replied immediately, sending me several articles on Alliance, Nebraska, and telling me about his work on the American Indian Council. By the time we met in September 1982 (while I was at the Pine Ridge Reservation collecting material for a course on Sioux history and culture), we had been corresponding by letter and telephone for six months. Mark drove me down to Alliance to visit with his family. In time our close friendship developed, and his daughters Connie and Hope adopted me as their mother. Their own mother, Emma Lone Wolf Monroe, had died in January 1982.

From the beginning I have felt that Mark had an important story to tell. Few people are aware of or hear about the kind of life Indians are living in off-reservation towns across America. Conditions are worst in the western states, particularly the Dakotas and Nebraska, where racial tensions run high and images of the Old West still prevail. When Mark decided in 1986 that he wanted to write his life story, I was pleased to be involved; we decided that he would relate his experiences into a tape recorder. Once he had begun producing tapes, my secretary, Mary Adamski, started to transcribe them; Mark and I filled in gaps and verified his recollections through telephone calls and letters, and during my visits to Alliance; we also poured over scrapbooks and photograph albums and talked with people who know Mark well. To be sure, we have excised repetition and edited for clarity, but our goal was always to convey Mark's story in his own words.

Born in a one-room log cabin on the Rosebud, South Dakota, Reservation, Mark grew up on the prairie in the close ties of the *tiospaye* (extended family). When he was ten and a half years old, the family moved to Alliance, a town situated in the western panhandle of Nebraska, ninety miles south of the Pine Ridge Reservation, now home of the Oglala Sioux. Fifty miles to the west lies Scottsbluff and Robidoux Pass, where the ruts made by pioneer wagons can still be seen. Not far away is Fort Robinson, the military outpost, now a museum, where the Sioux chief Crazy Horse was bayonetted to death. This is Willa Cather and Mari Sandoz country and the original home of several Indian tribes, of which the Sioux were the most numerous and best known.

Alliance was one of the railroad towns that sprang up on the prairie during the 1800s. Many of its 10,300 citizens are descendants of the early pioneers. People in this part of Nebraska are ranchers and farmers. Beans, sugar beets, potatoes, corn, wheat, and rye are the main crops. Alliance is also the off-reservation permanent residence of five hundred Sioux and a seasonal, fluctuating population from the Pine Ridge and Rosebud reservations across the border in South Dakota. Unemployment on these reservations is at an all-time high of 87 percent, and many Indians come to Alliance and neighboring towns looking for work during the summer months. It was during the 1930s that Indian migrants first came to the area to pick potatoes, sugar beets, and the Great Northern beans for the white farmers. This migrating Indian population is plagued with grave problems—alcoholism, drug addiction, lack of education and job training—which have added to the tensions between them and the townspeople.

Mark vividly recalls that when he and his family came to Alliance in the 1940s there were signs saying NO DOGS OR INDIANS ALLOWED—ONLY WHITE TRADE SOLICITED in the downtown store windows, and that he asked his mother, "Am I a dog?" His white friends could go to the local drugstore, but he had to wait outside until they brought him something to eat. The signs may be gone now, but racial animosity dies hard. Even today he notes, "If you go into a restaurant, they won't tell you as an Indian to leave, but you can sit there for over an hour and just not be served." People in this part of the country remember hearing about the Plains Indian wars, the burning of wagon trains and homesteads. They have seen Hollywood's slanted images of white western migration. For Mark, racism must be directly addressed, and people must be willing to sit down and discuss their differences. "It'll take time," he says, "to change people's hearts and minds."

Last year, an important meeting was held at the Alliance Public Library to address a number of problems facing the resident Indians and local white townspeople. A number of issues were discussed: Indian school student drop-outs, the need for an Indian school counselor, and the need for Indian teachers. Both sides also addressed the important social problems: lack of adequate housing and jobs, alcoholism, and racial tension. Mark Monroe was one of the key speakers and answered a number of questions posed by the audience. It is because of his hard work over the years that there are more hopeful signs in Alliance today. He has been able to persuade others that change is possible.

Carolyn Reyer

A·C·K·N·O·W·L·E·D·G·M·E·N·T·S

Grateful thanks go to

Delores Fleming, historian-editor, and Dr. Theodore Lustig, West Virginia University School of Journalism, for reading this manuscript and offering their insightful and helpful comments.

Mary Adamski, for her patience and hours spent typing and working on this manuscript.

Kenneth Lincoln, Mark's adopted brother and well-known author, for his willingness to write the Afterword to this book and to share reminiscences of his long association with Mark.

Janet Francendese, Executive Editor of Temple University Press, whose expertise and guidance in the final editing of this book were most appreciated.

Special thanks go to the Eberly College of Arts and Sciences of West Virginia University for providing partial funding toward the publication of this book.

AN I·N·D·I·A·N
in White America

C·H·A·P·T·E·R 1

CHILDHOOD MEMORIES
Wood, South Dakota

I have fond memories of my grandfather, John Monroe, whose Indian name was Long Time Sleep. He was a Cheyenne from the Cheyenne tribe in either Wyoming or Montana. Grandfather had very long black hair, which he wore in braids. In the early 1930s he was approached by members of the Buffalo Bill Wild West Show. He joined and toured Europe. Grandfather always sent back home to my grandmother packages of tobacco, perfume, and other luxuries totally unknown to local Indian people. What he did in the show was to be a member of an Apache Indian party attacking Buffalo Bill. When Grandfather came back home from Europe, I remember that he was really proud of himself. At that time I was very young—probably no more than two or three years old, as I was born in 1930. I was called Mark Stone Arrow after my mother's father, an Oglala Sioux. While in England, Grandfather saw the name Monroe, and sometime during those years he adopted that name for himself, which is the reason my father's name was Bill Monroe, and I became Mark Monroe.

At this time we lived way out in the country. The nearest town was Martin, South Dakota, and, if we wanted to do any shopping, we had to ride horseback or go in a wagon. Whenever I'd go over to my grandfather's house to eat, he would sit me up in a tall chair and give me the best parts of the chicken, the leg and the breast. He knew I wouldn't eat everything up, so he would wait until I'd get done and finish what was left. I think that was his way of getting more to eat himself. His name for me was "Black Mike," because I'm very dark and everything he gave me was black. I had a black chicken, a black horse, and I think even a black goat at that time. Grandfather was a happy, joking type of man, easy to get along with, and he loved me very much.

Sophie Mousseau, Grandfather's wife, came from the Pine Ridge Reservation in South Dakota, and she was an Oglala Sioux. I remember her as a very short, dark woman who always wore a black shawl. Wherever she would go, Grandmother would wrap me up in it and take me with her. One night we had a bad thunderstorm. Grandmother came to our tent and wrapped me up in her shawl. We just sat there together until the storm was over. All during this time, my mother and father were out looking for me and couldn't find me anywhere. Finally, they came to our tent, and there I was with my grandmother safe under her black shawl.

My father used to tell this story about my mother, Minnie Howard. Before they were married, she had lived in Rosebud; when they were first married and started having kids, we were living about 100 or 150 miles west of there, in Buzzard Basin. One day Mother got mad at my dad, and she started to walk back to Rosebud. As she started out, she looked behind her and there was my oldest brother, Butch, following her, then me, my black horse, my black goat, my black chicken, and my black dog. When she saw this, she started laughing and instead of continuing to pout, she came back to our place. Afterward my dad always said, "It's a good thing we had all those black animals because it saved my marriage!"

My mother's father was George Howard. He was also an Oglala Sioux from Pine Ridge Reservation, and he had a very interesting life. During the 1870s he was a scout for the United States Army and was stationed at Fort Robinson. My grandmother on my mother's side, Delphine Roubideaux, was also a very important person. She was related to Mr. Roubideaux, a Frenchman, who guided the early settlers to California over the Oregon Trail. In Scottsbluff, Nebraska, fifty-five miles west of us in Alliance, is the Robidoux Pass, which is named after him.

Some of the memories I have of my early years in Buzzard Basin are that it was a good life. We always had plenty to eat. My grandfather and my grandmother on my father's side were living with us. On my mother's side of the family, I had my grandmother, who had three brothers—Leo, Joe, and John—my other grandfathers. I also had Uncle Jimmy and Uncle Morris. Uncle Jimmy was married to a lady named Josephine, and Uncle Morris to Lillian. They all had large families (eight or ten children apiece), so we had quite a *tiospaye* (extended family). I don't remember our having any Indian neighbors. It seemed so isolated out there. Maybe it's because I was too young at that time to remember very much. My grandfather lived on kind of a little hill west of us. He had a large, long, log house with a wooden floor, and after we left our tent, we lived east of his place in the same type of dwelling, only ours was smaller. Across the creek from us was a white rancher who had a bunch of cattle. He used to keep his bulls in a pen right next to the creek. At night whenever those bulls would start fighting each other, I would get so scared. Just listening to them, the coyotes howling and all the noise the other animals were making, was frightening. I think my mother and dad were scared, too, but it was just the way of life out there on the prairie. We had to get used to it.

After my Dad got a job working on the dam, we moved to Wood, South Dakota, an off-reservation, white-dominated town on the perimeter of Rosebud Reservation. I was one of the few Indians living there out of a population of 200 people. We lived outside Wood, south of the railroad tracks in a log house with a wooden floor. When I say south of the tracks, I don't mean anything detrimental to the Indian people. At that time Indian people lived all over Wood. In those days the only thing a log house had was a wood stove, a table, chairs, and a bed. There were no modern conveniences like running water, electricity, and indoor plumbing. Early in the mornings, around six o'clock, I remember my mother getting up and cooking a large breakfast on the wood stove. She'd make pancakes or hot biscuits, fried eggs, and potatoes. Butch and I had the job of cutting wood every eve-ning and bringing it in to her. Nowadays, when I think back, I'm amazed how my mother was able to do all she did. She loved to cook and always managed to make good meals. Life is easy today in contrast, by golly.

As I remember them, my parents were two very hard-working, disciplined people, and I learned my discipline from them. My mother kept us boys at bay. Both our parents taught us respect for other people and not to cuss or tell lies. Indian people learn to honor and respect older members of the tribe. We respected our grandparents as well as our par-ents. My father was a man who respected women, and he taught me to be courteous toward them, to open doors for them and help a lady take off her coat. Later, when I was busing the elderly Presbyterian women to church, I did these things for them. They really liked it, and one lady told me she thought maybe this type of courtesy had gone out of style. "No," I told her, "my dad taught me to treat wom-en with utmost respect." I always admired him for being that way.

My mother and father spoke the Sioux language in our home, but my primary language was English. I wanted to learn to speak Sioux, so my mother began to teach me. But, if I didn't speak it perfectly immediately, she would ridicule me. This happened every time I tried, so I gave up. Years later when I joined the Army, there were five Indian men from the reservation in my platoon who could speak the lan-guage fluently. They did not seem to care what kind of mis-takes I made. From them, I learned to speak Sioux well enough to carry on a conversation, which I still can do today.

Grandpa Leo lived to the east of us in a tent. He never did live in a house. He always hunted and fished, and I think that's the way he made his living. He would get the commod-ities he needed from the tribe but hunted for his meat. One time, Grandpa Leo called me down to his place. So I went over there, and he had a large tub, the kind that you wash clothes in. He had the tub on top of the fire and was cooking something. He called me over and said, "Look what I got." He stuck a stick into the big tub, and there was a big turtle. It was an enormous one, which he probably got out of the large creek that ran east of Wood. I think this turtle was a foot or foot and a half in diameter, but the darn thing was still alive. The fire was burning underneath the tub so when he stuck the stick into it, the turtle grabbed ahold, and Grandpa just pulled him partly out. After I saw it, he put it back in the tub. He had some fish in there too, boiling with it. I don't think Grandpa washed them or anything, he just put them all in this big tub and cooked them. After a couple of hours of boiling, the turtle probably died and the fish did, too. Pretty soon, Grandpa pulled the tub away from the fire and reached in somehow to get the turtle out. It was evidently done. He did something with his knife on the sides of the turtle. He just lifted the shell right off this turtle like a man taking off his cap. I was really surprised when I saw that. You could tell it was a fish product because it was still kind of white, real white, and didn't look very tasty. When my grandfather Leo took the shell off, my grandmother came with her knife and started cutting it up. I always remember that the turtle really tasted good. She cut up some of the fish to go with it, and we ate that, too. I don't know how we refrigerated things in those days, but the next morning I went back over there to Grandpa Leo's tent, and my grandmother was cutting up more of the turtle into small pieces. She put them in a boiling pan with some hominy and cooked it all morning. Toward noon, she told me to go after my mother to come down and have dinner. She also made some fry bread. We came down and ate, and God, that soup was good! I always remember Grandpa Leo as a happy-go-lucky, very intelligent person. He was very protective of his brothers and his grandchildren. I think he was probably the original Indian that we hear and read so much about.

My Grandpa Joe lived close to Grandpa Leo and in a

tent also, but his tent was half wood. He had a wooden floor and wooden walls covered with a tent. During the wintertime he wouldn't have to worry about the snow coming in. I used to go down and see Grandpa Joe just so I could see his tent. It was real interesting.

Grandpa Johnny was the youngest of the three brothers. If I remember right, he was kind of a hell-raiser. He always went to town to drink or chase women. I don't remember too much about him. My three grandfathers all lived close together, but in their different tents in kind of a triangular arrangement.

My Grandmother Delphine, my mother's mother, lived in a nice house up on the main street, which consisted of two blocks of stores and filling stations and the rest were residential areas. She really loved her brothers and spent most of her time visiting them in their tents.

In the back of our house, to the west about a block away, my grandfather Carlos Gallineaux lived. (He was related to Grandmother Delphine on her father's side.) He was married, and I think at that time he was quite old. My mother used to tell me that he was a retired tribal judge, and everybody in town really respected him. One thing that always stands out in my mind is that Grandfather Gallineaux had two daughters. One was named Helen, the other Elizabeth. These daughters of his were probably thirty or thirty-five years old, and neither one of them was married. They had a lot of children but no husbands. My mother and I used to walk over there during the daytime, and she would visit with them. I always remember one time when we went to Elizabeth's house, she was cooking some cow hooves in the front of her home. Pretty soon she said, "Run outside and we'll eat." So we went out and took our plates to where she had a big pot cooking. She took the hoof out, laid it by the tray, and with a knife scraped on the edge of the hoof until it fell off. You could just see meat on the inside of it. I was really young at that time, about five, six, seven years old. The

whole pot she was cooking was full of hooves. I don't remember if they were cow or horse hooves, but everybody ate
them. I ate them, too, and they seemed all right. Now that I
think back, I say, "My God, what else?" It kind of amazes
me. They ate about every darn thing that you can imagine.
Nowadays, I don't think I'd eat something like a hoof, but it
seemed the thing to do then.

One of the vivid memories I have of Wood is of Rattlesnake Butte about seven miles outside town. On days when
the wind was blowing right, you could hear and smell these
snakes, big prairie rattlers, there were so many of them. They
rattled under the floor boards of our log house at night.
Whenever we'd go out to pick up eggs, we'd have to be
awfully careful as there might be a snake in the hen's nest. At
that time the railroad ran into Wood once a week on Satur-
days. There was a large ice house on the railroad property
with running water coming out of a pipe. My mother used to
send me down to get water, approximately a quarter of a
mile away from where we lived. One day she asked me to
take my little wooden wagon and cream cans down to haul
water. When I left, she was lying on a small cot inside our
house. I came back with the water and peeked in the screen
door. Right there under where Mother was lying, about six
inches from her face, was a large rattlesnake coiled to strike.
I didn't know what to do, so I ran the two or three blocks up
to my uncles' house and told them to come quickly. The
snake was still lying under Mother's nose when we got back.
Every time she breathed, it seemed like the snake would
breathe with her. My uncle had brought a rake. Very quietly
he opened the door, threw the rake on top of the snake, and
pulled it outside. Of course, when this happened, my mother
woke up with a start, imagined what had occurred, and was
really frightened. My two uncles killed the snake. The memory of this is so vivid that even today I sometimes dream
about snakes.

I don't remember too much about my dad in Wood.

He worked for the U.S. federal government in the 1930s and would get up at six o'clock every morning and come back about six o'clock in the evening. He made $1.50 a day. I don't think we were ever hungry or in want of anything, but with Dad's hours, I didn't get to see him much. So Butch, my oldest brother, was my father image. Butch taught me how to ride a horse, a bicycle, and how to fight. He took care of me. Butch was a very proud, athletic, cowboy type of person—a real macho man. At least that's the way I'd explain him today. He loved to trade wagons, bicycles, horses, anything he could lay his hands on.

When I went to school in Wood, I always had the feeling I was somehow better than the white kids in my classroom. I thought I could run faster, do everything better than they could. How I got this superior feeling, I don't know. One day we had races, and two of my friends, Kenny and Dwight, raced with me and they beat me. I couldn't get over it—that I was beaten by two white boys. I raced them again, and the same thing happened. I got really mad about this, and instead of being friends with these boys, I used to fight them. One day Kenny Troutman, my buddy, and I were playing out in the school yard when I got in a fight with another kid. I was really beating him up when Butch came along and stopped us. To this day, I wonder what would cause me to do a thing like this as I thought I got along pretty good with all the kids at school in spite of my superior feeling. Butch did, too. He was in junior high at this time and played on the football and basketball teams. He was a real good athlete and my idol. Everywhere Butch would go, I'd go with him. He had a spotted saddle horse he liked to ride, and whether he wanted me to or not, I'd jump right on back of his saddle if he was going swimming, and go along. Butch got mad at times. He had a girlfriend then, and sure didn't want me tagging along.

We used to have movies every Thursday night in Wood, and Butch loved to go. One night, he started out when Mom said, "You take Micky with you." Right below where we lived was a hill, and on it a little road you could turn off on and ride or walk a ways. Butch and I left and were speeding down the hill on his bike when we missed the turn. I remember our flying through the air and hitting the ground. Of course, there was nothing left of the bike. Every Thursday evening at this movie house, they would give out a prize. Whoever had the right number would win. My dad, mom, Butch, I, and my youngest brother, Bill, went to the shows. One night they called a number, and my dad, who was sitting right next to me, threw his hat in the air. He'd won the prize of $100, and, my gosh, $100 at that time was like a thousand or more today. All of Dad's friends who were in the theater came up and patted him on the back, and everybody walked him home that night. That night, all of our family, aunts, uncles, and Dad's cousins, had a big party. I always remember this.

Wood was such a frontier town at that time that it had a sheriff, Butch Larson. Anyway, he was the law. One day I was walking back from school, which was probably half or three-quarters of a mile from where we lived. We'd have to walk right down the main street, then kind of angle off southeast and across the railroad tracks to where our log house was. That day, when I was walking home and had gotten to the center of town, opposite the meat market, I looked up and saw an Indian man coming from the west right down the middle of the road. I don't remember now whether he had a rifle or shotgun or maybe just a stick in his hand. But I saw Butch Larson heading up the street toward him. They were both in the middle of the road. It reminds me of some of the old movies that we see nowadays where two cowboys face each other off and all of a sudden pull their pistols out and shoot one another down. I saw that happen. Butch Larson, our law, was coming down the street. He had a rifle in his hand, and when he got about a block away from this Indian, he raised his rifle and shot him down. The Indian guy's

name was Joe Metcalf, and he was one of our general hell-
raisers in Wood. He lived out in the country, but he would
come into town to raise a lot of heck. After I saw what happened, I went home and told Mom. Within a very few minutes the place was all crowded with people who wondered
what was going on. My mother ran down the street. I never
did know or hear what provoked the attack. To this day,
that shooting incident remains fresh in my memory. Every
time I see a movie, I always think about it. It gives you an
idea of what a wild and woolly kind of town Wood, South
Dakota, was.

We had a jail made out of blocks; it was no more than
sixteen feet wide by about twenty feet long, separated in the
middle by a wall. The jail was set out in the middle of town
with nothing around it. It was on one block by itself and very
prominent. I remember we kids used to play around it, and
we'd peek in. There were large bars on the door, and I suppose the reason for that middle wall was to keep the women
on one side and the men on the other. There were no toilet
facilities, no running water, or anything in that jail. All it had
was two cots on one side and two cots on the other side and
a small mattress. Whenever Butch Larson would arrest anybody, well, he would just take them down there and throw
them in the jail, I suppose, until the next day. I remember
that jail very well.

My mother's youngest brother, Uncle Jimmy, and my
Aunt Josie drank quite a bit. They were general hell-raisers.
We had a bar in Wood where everybody would go to dance,
drink, or do whatever they wanted to do. Every Sunday, rain
or shine, my mother used to like to go to church. So my dad
would hitch up our team of horses, and we'd drive approximately seven miles out in the country to the Catholic church.
When we got back one Sunday, I was walking around this
jail, which was about two or three blocks from where we
lived. There was smoke coming out of the building. Butch
and I ran down there to see what was going on, and here my

Aunt Josie was in one side of the jail, and Uncle Jimmy was in the other. What had happened, I guess, was when Josephine woke up, she was really mad and set the mattress on fire. By that time, quite a few people had come to see what was going on.

One summer, when I was six or seven and Butch was ten or eleven, we began going to St. Francis to the Indian mission school, which was probably about thirty or thirty-five miles away from where we lived in Wood. The father of the Catholic church would want all the Indian children to attend summer school for two weeks so that we would learn about God and the Catholic beliefs. Dad took me and Butch to St. Francis and left us there. St. Francis is a small town, too; I think it was smaller than Wood. The only thing they had there was a large Indian school. Butch and I got separated. He stayed with the big boys, and I stayed with the little boys. Every morning about ten o'clock, the fathers and the brothers would bring in hot buns and just stand there and throw them out to the crowd. One way or another, you could reach up and get a hot bun. I didn't like it there too much because there were a lot of kids who did nothing but fight. They were all Indian children, and I thought, maybe we came to school to learn how to fight. You just kind of had to be careful what you said or who you looked at because they'd start fighting right away. The Catholic priest and brothers and sisters would run around breaking up the fights.

We stayed there two weeks. We went up on a Sunday and were supposed to come back on a Sunday. The Sunday that we were supposed to come home, Butch and two of his friends from Wood decided to walk home. One of them was named Harvey Dustrude and the other's name was Dick Moran. They were Butch's age and about his size. Butch came up to me and said, "Mick, Harvey and Dick and I are going to walk home. We are going to hitchhike." At that time there weren't too many cars around, so I didn't know how in the world they would get home. But they left early

Sunday morning right after church. Nobody seemed to care about it, and I didn't hear any of the priests looking for them. So I waited and waited until about four or five o'clock in the evening when Dad drove up. He had an old Model T, and he was the only Indian in Wood who had a car. Dad came and said, "Well, where's Butch?" I told him they walked home that morning and left at seven. Dad really got mad. We came on home, and about an hour later Butch, Harvey, and Dick were walking down the railroad tracks coming from the west. Evidently, they got on the wrong road and went north instead of going northeast. Boy, I tell you, Dad was really mad at those guys. I think also that he was really happy they made it back safely because he was worried about them. The summer after that, we went back to St. Francis school again, but I sure dreaded it.

I remember a Catholic church seven miles out of town where we had all of our Christmas days and nights. During Christmas time we would go out there, and Dad would pitch a tent for us, and we'd stay for the Christmas holidays. There were a whole bunch of tents camped around the church. They had a large meeting hall that I think all the Indian men built for the Catholic church. Inside it, they would hold Christmas dinner and meetings. We would bring all our Christmas presents, cakes, cookies, and pies. On Christmas Eve everybody would open up their Christmas presents, drink coffee, and eat pie and cake. It was more than a family affair; it was for the whole community. All the Catholics who lived in Wood and the surrounding areas would come. It was just a lot of people. About 100–150 Indians would go to these Christmas and Easter parties. Santa Claus would come on Christmas Eve. Nowadays what we do is just get our families together, have our Christmas dinner and Christmas Eve, and give away presents on Christmas morning. But in those days, everybody did it together.

One particular Christmas Eve I always remember, I got a present. They called out names, and Santa Claus would come give gifts to the children. He called my name, and I went up there. He had a great big box for me. When I opened it up, there was a brand-new bus, and I had that bus clear up until I was seventeen or eighteen years old. As for games, I think the only thing that Butch and I played with were bone horses made out of part of the hoof. A horse's hoof breaks up into about four or five different toe-like bones. These dried-out bones were what we used to play with. We called them bone horses. Butch would get those old match boxes and make a little wagon, and he would take large buttons and make the wheels out of them. Then he'd take a stick and use it for the tongue of the wagon. That's all Butch and I had to play with. So when I got this bus, I thought I was kind of "king of the kids." I was so proud of it.

Another of my good memories of Wood is of sheep-herding. Butch was always a go-getter, so he got a job on a sheep ranch right under Rattlesnake Butte and worked out there in the summers. One summer my mother told him to take me with him, which he wasn't too happy about, but he did. Butch was making a dollar a day herding approximately six thousand sheep. The rancher and his wife, the Weavers, were kind people. We slept on the cot in the bunkhouse. In the mornings Mrs. Weaver would have good breakfasts of orange juice and pancakes; dinners and suppers were also big meals. I always remember the good eats. In the bunkhouse Mrs. Weaver had brooders of baby turkeys, which she raised. One night when Butch and I were lying on the cot, I looked up and saw the biggest bull snake you'd ever see in your life crawling toward our bed. I jumped up and said, "Butch, there's a big snake crawling toward you; you better get up!" "Aw, leave it alone. That's their pet," Butch replied. This bull snake, I swear, was six feet long and probably three or four inches in diameter. He just crawled around and lay under our bed, so I had a heck of a time getting to sleep that night. The next day Chet Weaver told me he kept that bull snake on the ranch to kill the rattlesnakes. Well, everywhere I'd go in the rancher's house, in the kitchen or to his living room, there was this old bull snake lying there. We had only outhouses, and when you'd go there, the snake would be lying in the building or in front. I was scared of the darn thing, but I had to learn to live with him.

Mr. Weaver had a ram sheep without any horns who stayed around the ranch house. He was a good ram, but once in a while he'd get a mean streak. My job was to help Mrs. Weaver around the house, keep her yard clean, and in the afternoons I'd help Butch walk around with the sheep. One morning I heard Mrs. Weaver hollering and hollering, so I ran around the house, and there she was in the outhouse. The old ram wouldn't let her out, and he was butting the door. I found Mr. Weaver out working some horses in the corral and told him what had happened. He came, got the old ram, and tied him up. It wasn't funny at the time, but looking back it seems like it was real comical.

On this ranch Mr. Weaver had horses and cows along with his six thousand sheep. The sheep would graze right up into Rattlesnake Butte. In the evenings, when the sheep wouldn't come in, Butch, who was a regular cowboy, had to ride out toward the Butte and bring them in. I got to go with him. He had a large black whip he called his "black snake" made out of leather, and if we'd see a rattlesnake up there when driving our sheep home, Butch would just whip out that "black snake" of his and cut the rattler's head off. He was just good at everything on the ranch, and I admired him and wanted to be the same way, but somehow I never could be. I was too scared, too afraid.

One night, the last summer that Butch and I worked out there, Mr. Weaver said, "I'll take you boys home in the morning." Butch and I got to talking. "Heck, let's surprise everybody and walk home," Butch said. It was totally dark, and the ranch was out in the middle of nowhere, about seven miles from our home. We made it, but we went into town first. There was a saloon there where we knew my dad always went to play poker after work. We peeked in the window, and there he was with some other people from around Wood. Dad saw us, ran out, and said, "How in the heck did you guys get back into town?" We told him we walked. Right away the next day, my dad rode over to Mr. Weaver's house to tell him we got home safely. Mr. Weaver was checking on us, too, and so he met Dad halfway.

One summer when we worked for Mr. Weaver, he had these really beautiful greyhounds. I worked all summer until the day school started, and Mr. Weaver used to buy my school clothes for me: cowboy boots, levis, shirts, caps, and coats. I suppose that was my pay. One of his prize greyhounds had puppies, and seeing how much I liked them, Chet Weaver gave me the best one out of the litter. The next day he drove Butch and me into town. Butch was sitting in the front seat of the pickup with him while I was in the back with all those greyhound puppies and their mother. When we got home, my mother got mad at first when she saw me, but then she started crying when I got out with my little greyhound puppy. I was very happy, and I kind of figured this was my whole summer's salary, as these hounds were worth hundreds of dollars!

The most vivid memory I have of sheep-herding occurred toward fall, probably around the middle of August. Chet Weaver would take five or six hundred sheep to market in Winner, South Dakota, about thirty-five miles from his ranch. In those days they didn't have trucks to haul them, so one day he asked Butch if I could take the sheep to market. Butch came over and told me, "Mick, you get ready; you're going to herd these sheep into Winner!" Mr. Weaver had an awful good sheep dog—she was a beauty. One morning, we took off walking very early—me, the sheep dog, and hundreds of sheep. We walked all day long, and the dog was so well trained that all I had to do was walk behind the sheep and she would keep them going straight. That night when we stopped, Mr. Weaver and Butch came and bedded down with us. I suppose we must have covered fifteen or twenty miles a day because it took us only two days to reach Winner. When we got into town, the dog just herded the sheep right into the pen. After Mr. Weaver and Butch arrived, he took us to a drugstore. It was the first time I ever saw one with a soda fountain. Mr. Weaver bought us sodas and pop, and it sure was nice. Winner was a large town with between 1,000 and 1,500 people, and I was surprised how big it was. Mr. Weaver seemed to be very proud of me herding all those sheep into town for him. It sure gave me a good feeling.

When we were going to school in Wood, one day my dad came home and said, "Let's get packed up; we're going to Nebraska." That night, my mom asked him, "Why are we going to Nebraska?" "Well," he said, "I've got a good job out there. We're going to pick potatoes for a lady named Mrs. Worley." So we packed up, and the next day the truck stopped to pick us up. It was in the fall of 1941. When the truck came, two other families—one my Uncle Morris's and the other Uncle Jimmy's—with their clothes and whatever else they could take with them, were on board. We left. The truck drove and drove, and in a few places we would stop to eat and then get back on again. Finally, we came to Alliance, Nebraska. Everything changed for us there. Many times I was to look back on those days in Wood and remember how good our life had been.

C·H·A·P·T·E·R II

HARD TIMES
Alliance, Nebraska

After we arrived in Alliance, the first place we worked was on a large potato farm. There must have been fifty to sixty tents and the same number of families. I was probably ten or eleven years old. They asked us if we'd had any experience with horses and cows. Butch right away said, "Yeah, we know how to do it," so we both got good jobs. Mrs. Worley told us, "You boys go out to the barn there, and each of you get a horse. Mick, you can start herding sheep, and Butch, you can take care of the cows and horses." She gave me a large spotted horse that was so tall I could hardly get up on her. Whenever I'd stop somewhere, I'd go against a fence so I could get off and on easier.

Everybody was working hard on this farm making good money, fifty dollars a week, which my dad said was four times what he was making when we lived in South Dakota. Then the war broke out. Right away, they started building an air base in Alliance. One day my dad went into town and signed up for a job working there. As I remember, it was either May or June 1942.

When we moved into Alliance, we went to South Alliance, which was divided from the main part of town by a large viaduct. There were five hundred Indian tents lined up like army tents in South Alliance in those days, with two to three thousand Indian people living in them—all working at the air base. Many of them came from Pine Ridge, Rosebud, and neighboring towns.

When my dad started to work out there, Butch did, too. He was about fifteen years old, but I think he lied about his age so he got a job with the Civil Service. Both Dad and

Butch received checks for fifty-four dollars a week, and were they proud!

Living in tents was really rough. We had no place to take a shower, no inside toilet, no conveniences. My mother would bathe us in tubs and wash us the best she could in the mornings. We used to have to go to the bathroom about a block away to an outside toilet. We lived in these tents for five or six years before we even got a shack.

I always remember the one morning during the wintertime, when I woke up quite early and I tried to peek out of the flap of the tent. The snow was at least two and one half or three feet deep. It really scared me because I was wondering, how are we going to get outside the tent? I looked around, and my mother and father, sisters, and brothers were still sleeping in the tent so evidently this was quite early in the morning. I remember I woke my dad up and told him, "Dad, looks like we won't be able to get out because the snow is too deep." We were all sleeping on the ground. My dad had put tarp down to cover the earth, and we all had our quilts and blankets piled on top of it where we slept at night. In the middle of the tent Dad had put a fifty-gallon barrel that he had cut in half and made a stove out of it in which he burned wood. We got our heat from a stovepipe that ran directly through the ceiling of our tent. I remember back to those rough days, and I always wonder how we were able to manage to live through them. When my dad got up that morning, he put on his clothes and started shoveling the snow away from our tent so we could get up, go out, and go to school—whatever we had to do. This experience is something that really bothered me, and it remains very clear in my memory.

The first day Bill and I started Grandview Elementary School, my mom took us and enrolled us. Bill is four years younger than I am. We boys went to the school yard. There was another Indian kid there named Standing Soldier. All the white children came and looked us over like we were something different. I don't think the children themselves had ever heard of Indians or knew what one looked like. Anyway, for about fifteen minutes they just stood there, looked at us, and then all of a sudden the fighting began. It was kind of a horrible experience for us. First, we were treated like we were something completely different, like we didn't belong there, and finally, after they found out that we were Indians, well, some of the guys came up and started a fight. Bill and I remember that when we went back and forth to school, we had a fight in the morning, at noontime, during recess, and after school as well. We got to be pretty tough kids!

At that time the state of Nebraska evidently had a law stating that all children had to be in school until they were sixteen years of age, so what the city school system did was take all Indian children regardless of age and put them in one room. It was called the Opportunity Room. Bill and I were very fortunate; we managed to escape being put there. My future wife, Emma, however, and all of my friends were in there. Basically, what they did was just attend school. They weren't taught anything. They weren't given a report card. They weren't advanced from one grade to another. They just stayed in this room, drew pictures, and marked on the blackboard. My wife was in this room for seven years. When she started school, she was in the fifth grade. When she got out, she was still in the fifth grade. There was no advancement, no recognition of her going to school all those years.

I suppose this was the white school system's way of obeying the state law to keep Indian children in school without teaching them. They asked me to go into this room, but I said no. I told them I would rather go along and be in the regular classes. I was going into junior high at this time. The Indian children were really happy they didn't have to learn anything—just put in seven or eight hours at school. They were always laughing at Bill and me because we attended regular classes, advanced, and did everything that was normal for school children to do. We were glad we did because we did get educated. In our modern-day world, I'm always surprised that something like keeping Indian children in one room for seven years could ever happen, and I have always questioned it.

When we moved to Alliance, we soon found out there was a ladder of racism. First were the white people, then the Mexicans, then the blacks, and, finally, the Indians. You see, when the American Indian first came to Alliance, the Negro was last on the ladder, but then what happened was the Indian population was discriminated against by blacks, Mexicans, and whites alike. When Bill and I started school, the first children we got in trouble with were the Negro kids. I think this was the first time that black people ever felt superior to anybody.

When the Indian people came into Alliance, the businesses in the downtown district put up signs saying "No Indians or dogs allowed." This meant we couldn't go into restaurants or drugstores, only the grocery and food stores. When we did, we had to go in large numbers for fear of being beaten up.

In eighth grade I had some good white friends—people who understood and couldn't see any racial barrier. In eighth grade we used to either take lunch or walk home for a meal. A couple of my friends would go down to the drugstore called Hested's in Alliance. In the window was a large sign, "No Indians or dogs allowed." So my two friends would walk into the store, order themselves a sandwich and a malt, whatever, and eat it. On their way out they'd bring me a sandwich or pop, which I'd have to eat outside. Sometimes, when I was out there waiting for them, I'd wonder what in the world could cause people to do something like this to another human being. You see, with this superior feeling I still had from attending elementary school in Wood, South Dakota, I never could understand why my two white friends were better than I was. As I have said, I fought a number of times, physically and mentally, and always thought about those other Indian children. How did they manage?

What got me through ninth grade was my superior feeling. You had to have this type of attitude to survive; those who didn't have it ended up in the Opportunity Room. I wanted to get through high school because I knew the meaning of an education—especially in Alliance. What caused me to quit in ninth grade was that I had to fight someone practically every day—a black, a Mexican, or a white kid. It was getting to the point where it was just too hard on my mother and father. When Bill and I came home from school beaten up, they were scared. I was scared. It was something that should not have happened to anybody.

What brought matters to a head one morning was that Allen Moore, the son of the elementary school's principal, and I were sitting close together in class. He kept kicking me from behind. As you know, there are no backs to the desk chairs in junior and senior high. When my back got so sore I couldn't stand it any more, I stood up and hit Allen right in the eyes, breaking his glasses. The teacher hadn't seen any of this happen so, before she did, I got up and ran home. I told my mother about it. That evening, Allen and his father came to our house and told my dad we'd have to pay for Allen's glasses or be taken to court. Dad said, "My son is quitting school, and I'm not going to pay for your son's glasses, so get going before I start to beat you up." Dad lived a tough life, and he was a fighter. He felt with my quitting school, I was losing more than Allen did.

My father told us he could not make enough money for us to move back to Wood, so we had to make the best of everything. My memory of Alliance and of South Alliance where the Indian people had to live is of very bad experiences. Why, where, how did this racism start? I'd never heard of it before. When we lived in Wood, there was some racial tension, but it wasn't as bad as this. In Alliance we were just different, and we couldn't do anything right.

When we were living in our tents in South Alliance, there were a lot of blacks at the air base. At night black MPs would be standing at the viaduct that separated South Alli-

ance from Main Street. They were there evenings from nine
o'clock on to be sure no one left our tent city to go into
town. Some of the people who did sneak out were caught,
taken to city court, and fined. During the years after I had
seen how the Jewish people were treated in Germany by the
Nazis, I compared their ghettoes to the life we were living in
Alliance. We Indians fought back the best way we could.
Every Indian felt "this is my country, I have the right to live
here regardless of my dark skin. I'm going to fight for that
right no matter what the conditions are." As I was growing
up, I never realized that, at one time, the federal government
had wanted to kill off all the Indians, just as Hitler had
wanted to get rid of the Jews. I later learned about the opening of the West. Although we no longer have signs forbidding
us to go into public places, Alliance still has racial barriers.
They are less obvious, but we can feel them.

During my school days some of the white children
asked what it was like to live in a tent, and I'd tell them how
rough it was. They had a hard time believing it. My childhood friends would never come over to South Alliance to
visit us. It was degrading to them to do something like that,
and that hurt. We had our Indian relations living around us,
mothers, fathers, grandparents, aunts, uncles, and cousins, so
it actually didn't make too much difference to us. The older
people were able to ignore the racism—all they wanted to do
was make a living, get along, and survive. So Bill and I just
continued to fight, continued to attend school.

During the summer months I wanted to make money
somehow. I used to ride my bicycle out to where my dad
worked at the air base to take his lunch to him and visit all
the PXs and the hospital. Knowing how the soldiers liked
everything neat and orderly and their shoes and boots shiny, I
made up a little box with brush, rags, and polish, and I set
up a shoe-shining business. I rode uptown, stood in front of
the canteen, and shined shoes for the soldiers. Well, they'd
give me fifty cents or a dollar, and many nights I'd come

home with at least twenty-seven or thirty dollars in my pockets for four or five hours' work. So, I was making more money shining shoes than my dad was at the air base. Pretty soon the Mexicans, blacks, and some of the white kids saw me doing this so they started to do it, too. Finally, we had more shoe-shine boys than we had soldiers. Well, instead of shining shoes in town, I decided to ask permission of the major out at the air base if I could come to the PX, and he said it would be okay, so I moved my shoe-shine business out there. It was sure a good way to make money.

Not everything in Alliance was bad—there were a lot of good things, and I think it was just what a man, woman, or child made of that life. My mother, father, two sisters, and two brothers survived—my two sisters, Lillian and Mary Ann, were both born in Alliance. Dad continued to work at the air base. As soon as I had dropped out of school for a few months, I got a job with a nursery trimming trees, digging them up and planting them. I learned a pretty good trade doing that and was able to continue for a while.

But in the winter months of 1949 there were no jobs in Alliance and nothing for inexperienced people to do. At that time, I was eighteen years old, so I joined the Army and was sent to Fort Riley, Kansas. Butch had joined in 1945 and was with the occupation troops in Japan, but he was discharged in 1948 and came back to Alliance. He never mentioned that there was racism also in the Army. I was placed in an all-white platoon; I was the only Indian in it until they moved in about fifteen other Indian soldiers from the reservation.

The black people had their own regiments and divisions, and kept completely away from the white people. That's when I first understood the blacks' plight in the United States. I heard they were treated worse in the South. When I saw that the Army trained these black soldiers separately and kept them separate, it kind of made me "come to" for a moment. I thought, well, look, there are some other people being treated just like Indians are.

When I joined up in 1949, the Army let you enlist for one year and go into enlisted reserves for five years. I did that and went successfully through basic training and through leadership training school at Camp Carson, Colorado. In January 1950 I was discharged and entered the active reserves. We had to attend a meeting every two weeks, but all of this counted toward retirement time. I liked the Army, I really did. After being discharged and returning to Alliance, I found there were no jobs. Even my dad who was working was barely making a living.

In 1946 I had met and started to go with Emma Lone Wolf. Her parents lived the same way mine did in tent city, and she had attended the Opportunity Room. We had a lot in common. The first moment I saw her, I fell in love with her. All the time I was in the Army, and especially after I got discharged, I remember Emma, my mom and dad telling me "something is going to break loose and you'll get a job somewhere."

Toward the end of August 1950, Butch and I worked odd jobs in Alliance just about any place that we could get one, and we started working for a farmer about four miles out of Alliance. Butch and I learned how to cultivate beets. Butch would go into town at dinner time to get the mail or some lunch for us. One day when he returned, he had a letter from the U.S. Army stating that I had to be in Omaha, Nebraska, at 7:00 A.M. the next morning. I really didn't know what to do because I didn't have enough money to go to Omaha. It kind of scared me, too, but Butch and I told the farmer, showed him the letter I received, and he gave us the rest of the day off.

My mother and father had gone to Rapid City, South Dakota, where they were visiting Mom's sister. Butch and I went home, and I got enough money together for the train ticket to Omaha. That afternoon I started cleaning up, getting some clothes ready, and about 9:00 P.M. I boarded the train and headed for Omaha, where I took my physical examination, which I passed. We were allowed three days at home, and then we were to get our traveling orders. I knew our destination was going to be Fort Lewis, Washington. I came back to Alliance and told Butch what was going to happen. Butch, his wife, Priscilla, and their youngest son Bobby were the only ones who were at home. My mother and father, brother Bill, and sisters Lillian and Mary Ann were still in Rapid City. When I left for Fort Lewis, my girlfriend Emma and her folks, Butch, Priscilla, and their children all saw me off at the train.

It was a very lonely parting because except for Butch my own family wasn't there. I knew I was going to Korea.

C·H·A·P·T·E·R III

A SECOND GUNNER
Korea

During the time I was first on active duty in the Army, from January 1949 to January 1950, I worked in a heavy weapons company. My job was the second gunner on an 81-millimeter mortar. The second gunner is the man who drops the rounds into the tube. My MOS (military occupational specialty) was 4812. After being called back, when I was taking refresher course training at Fort Lewis, I trained on 81-millimeter mortars again. After our training period was over, we were immediately sent to Fort Lawton in Seattle, Washington.

When we arrived there, I think we were all under the impression that we were going by ship to Japan and Korea. We were taken to a place called Pier 91 in Seattle. We must have stayed there at least four days. Somewhere in that four-day period the orders were changed, and we flew out of Seattle. I remember it was Saturday night, and Saturday night had always been kind of a special night for me at home. Even during the time I was in the Army, Saturday night was always the night that we would go uptown, take our girlfriend out, or go to the drive-in movie. It was kind of special. That Saturday night, we were at McCord Field in Seattle. Forty to forty-five men were assigned to fly in the plane. It may have been more, but that number seems to stick in my mind. We put on our full combat equipment: our rifles, field packs, helmet with helmet liner, and steel helmet. We were prepared for combat when we entered the plane. It was a very lonely night that Saturday night sometime in the early or middle part of September, as I could imagine what everyone was doing at home. I think every soldier who was leaving that night felt the same way I did, and I saw tears in a lot of the guys' eyes.

Most of the soldiers who got on the plane were about my age, maybe some of them eighteen or nineteen years old. They were very young men; no one was any older than twenty-one. We all knew that we were going directly to Japan and Korea for combat and were fearful that we would never see our families again. Our first stop was at Anchorage, Alaska, where we got off and went to eat supper. You could feel the cold as soon as you got off the plane. I didn't enjoy the meal, and I don't think anybody else did either. Then we got back on the plane.

Our next landing point was an island called Shemya Island. After I was discharged and became a civilian again, I looked for Shemya Island on the map but could never find it. It was such a tiny island. When we got off at Shemya and were eating again, some of the Air Force personnel there told us that Russia was so close that on clear days they could hear the Russian soldiers and sailors training across the expanse of ocean between Shemya Island and Russia. When we heard this, I think it made all of our men fearful again because we were getting so close to our destination. We all boarded the plane again, and our next stop was Tokyo, Japan.

When we got to Tokyo, one of the first things we saw was Mount Fujiyama. I remembered reading in geography books about Mount Fujiyama, and when I saw it, I thought it was very beautiful. We were flying in clouds, but we could still see the top of it. When we landed in Tokyo and they opened the door, the first thing I remember was the terrible, foul smell that was in the air. I was told later on that this was the human excrement that Japanese people used as fertilizer on their farms.

When I got to Japan, I was very much in awe of everything I saw. We were first taken to Camp Drake for orientation and another issue of clothing; we more or less got used to being in Japan. The stay in Camp Drake couldn't have

been more than four or five days before we went to a place
called Beppu. In Beppu we were assigned to our divisions,
regiments, and companies. This is where I was separated
from all the friends I had made on the way to Japan and in
Camp Drake. To my surprise, I was put into a company
where there were only two Americans to a squad. Normally,
a squad consisted of twelve men, with a squad leader. In our
company all the rest were Republic of Korea (ROK) soldiers.

As soon as I saw these men, I knew that we were at a
disadvantage because we could not even communicate with
them. They spoke Korean, and none of us knew their language. Some of the things that I saw seemed very comical.
For instance, when we would line up for our chow in the
morning, these ROK soldiers would take their canteen cups,
and when the cooks put coffee in them, they put their cereal
in the coffee and ate it that way. I saw a lot of them throw
away their eggs, bacon, and milk.

I think I was the lowest ranked man in the American
part, and it was my duty to train these Koreans how to eat
their breakfast, dinner, and supper. I worried about what
would ever happen if we got into combat with these guys, because working with an 81-millimeter mortar takes complete
teamwork or else the gun will not operate correctly. I just
couldn't communicate with them. I am an American Indian,
so there wasn't much difference in the way we looked. I think
they kind of liked me right away for that reason, but still,
communicating and teaching them anything was impossible. I
just showed them what to do.

I was very apprehensive about these ROK soldiers. To
me, it seemed like nobody cared. I thought to myself, that's
the way we're going to go into combat, and that's the way
we did. When we got into Beppu, I was immediately placed
as a first gunner on an 81 mortar. I suppose someone in the
regiment read my MOS and immediately figured I had first-
gunner experience. The first-gunner position is a very intri-
cate job. You have to do all the sighting. You have to listen

to the forward observer's report. When he reports to you, you set the sight. Once the sight is set, you have your second gunner drop the round. I was no expert at this job, but I was assigned it anyway. I told our squad leader, Corporal Gossett, that I was not a first gunner, but it didn't seem to make any difference; I was still going to go into combat in that position.

Nowadays, when I think about what happened in Korea, I wonder if some of the instances where we didn't perform as well as we should have was because the ROK soldiers did not have any experience in the 81 mortar. They absolutely didn't know anything about it, and we didn't have enough time to train them properly. I think we only had a week or a week and a half in Japan. To me, that wasn't enough. They were just civilians who were picked off the street, put into the South Korean army, and sent away to train with us. But at the time I figured, well, I might as well convince myself that I was a first gunner and that I could handle the job. We practiced on the 81 mortar using dummy rounds in Japan. Corporal Gossett seemed to have a lot of experience with it, and I felt very comfortable working with him.

After we supposedly trained these ROK soldiers and I was classified as the first gunner on the 81 mortar with Corporal Gossett as our squad leader, we were sent to Kokura, Japan. At Kokura we were outfitted with cold-weather clothing and prepared the next morning to board ship and head for Korea. I don't know what happened to the ROK soldiers on the ship. They must have been kept somewhere else on board. A lot of our young soldiers really got seasick after they ate, but that's something that never bothered me, for which I was thankful. I pulled guard duty in the bottom of the ship guarding some of the trucks and jeeps and weapons carriers. We would pull four hours on guard and then eight off during a twelve-hour period. It was a very long, lonely trip.

On the morning we landed in Korea, we drove the weapons carrier that was assigned to us off the ship. Corporal Gossett, a driver, myself, and two or three ROK soldiers went into Wonsan; we could see that it had been shelled. I was told later on that the Marines had made a landing there. You could see flyers, smoke, and all the tell-tale signs of prior combat.

We drove to a spot and got reorganized. The rest of our ROK troops, who were riding in the truck behind our weapons carrier, caught up with us. Everything seemed to be very disorganized. Our whole regiment started working its way into the mountains, where, I was told later, the Marines had fought their way through. We saw bodies of North Korean soldiers lying along the side of the road and became very frightened about what was coming next. Our company, battalion, and—we hoped—our regiment continued up the mountainside.

Finally we arrived at our perimeter, which was on the top, where I met a young Marine who had been with one of the troops that had fought in Wonsan and gone this far into enemy territory. He was about my age. I noticed that he was shot, but he didn't seem to care. We talked no more than half an hour, as he had to rejoin his company to continue fighting elsewhere. This was probably his first time in combat, and he didn't seem to be very afraid, so this kind of made me feel better.

Our company stayed at this perimeter. From there, we would launch combat patrols into enemy territory. I noticed that every day our rifle companies would go out and probe for the enemy. Many of these combat patrols would ask for the assistance of our 81 mortar. This would mean that any other squad in our company might get picked to accompany the rifle company. We were kind of a backup to rifle companies and to whoever was on combat duty in that particular area.

We were all afraid. I was very afraid, and I think even

the officers were afraid. We had only one officer whom I
knew and saw many times. He was our company leader, a
lieutenant. The other white man was Corporal Gossett. I
think there were a few other first gunners on the one mortar
in our squad, and I met them. They were in the same position
we were. They had ROK soldiers who made up the rest of
their squads. Everyone was very fearful because I think they
felt the same thing I did: How in the world could we ever do
combat with such inexperienced men, men we couldn't even
communicate with, and didn't even know?

On November 23, 1950, which was Thanksgiving Day,
word got out that we were going to have a hot Thanksgiving
dinner. Everybody was really happy about this. We had been
eating canned C rations that were left over from World War
II. Everyone was afraid to light fires at night or even during
the daytime, so we ate most of our meals out of cans, cold.
Just once in a while we would have a hot meal, but we
would have to go quite a way from our gun emplacement to
get it.

But on that Thanksgiving our combat patrol was sent
out, and my squad was the one accompanying the rifle company. I always remember marching along a long, winding
road in the mountains. I was carrying the bipod of the mortar, which comes in three pieces, a bipod, a tube, and a base
plate. Each one of these pieces weighed approximately thirty-
five or forty pounds, or maybe a little bit more. We were
marching along, and all of a sudden we came under attack.
At that time, everyone was so scared and disorganized that it
was kind of hard to tell what was happening. I think we en-
gaged parts of the North Korean army.

There are a lot of things that I can say about our being
under attack that day. I love my country, and I loved the
Army, but I have to say that there was a lot of confusion, a
lot of disorganization, and a lot of fear. What caused this
was that the rifle company we were backing up and our
squad had never worked together before or actually ever been

in combat. I don't think we did things normally, and many men got killed.

Our forward observer, Corporal Gossett, whom I liked very much and who became a very good friend, was way in the front of our gun. Somehow Corporal Gossett and I never got in touch through our walkie-talkie communications. I don't know why he could not communicate with our gun. So without his communication, our gun was absolutely useless; without his firing direction, I didn't know where to fire, when to fire, or what types of ammunition to use. What I did was to place our gun up and fire over the heads of our troops, hoping that I would not hit any of them. However, we were overrun, and I dismantled the gun. When I looked around, there were no more ROK troops behind me because they just ran away as soon as they saw the enemy coming and firing. They were not there to help us. So I carried the bi-pod with the sight and retreated.

Anyway, it was on November 23, 1950, I was wounded in action and shot in the left hand. I was also wounded in the upper right thigh. I was very afraid, but I didn't know that I was shot until I was organized with our group again. When we were in combat, we were a completely disorganized group, and I don't think anyone knew what they were doing or what they were supposed to do. It was just frightening. In looking back, I'm sure now that if we had all been Americans in our squads and companies, this fear wouldn't have been so prevalent. But with our thinking that we could not depend on or work with the ROK army, a lot of fear and distrust resulted.

The weather was so cold that it had a numbing effect. When we arrived back at the point where we left our truck and got aboard to return to our perimeter, the sergeant who was in charge came over and said I was bleeding. A lot of the other guys were bleeding, too. When we returned to our medical aid station in our perimeter, we were all undressed, our wounds were treated, and we lay in cots.

About two o'clock in the morning Corporal Gossett returned. I remember talking to him explicitly about what happened. Corporal Gossett told me that he was way out in
front of our combat patrol when the enemy overran him. The
soldiers from the rifle company were immediately killed, dis-
armed, undressed, and just shot to pieces by the enemy. During this time Corporal Gossett hid and watched everything
that happened. Our soldiers were just mutilated out in the
frontal area of our combat patrol. Somehow, Corporal Gossett came back over the entire twenty-five miles from where
we were during that night. He told me that the only danger
he encountered was that when he got back to our perimeter,
our soldiers nearly shot him, fearing that he was the enemy.
But he made it back, and that was the last time I saw Corporal Gossett.

From our perimeter aid station, we were taken to another one in Korea, and from there we were sent to Tokyo.

From the field hospital, I was taken to Wonsan, then to
Seoul, and finally by airplane back to Tokyo, where I stayed
in another hospital. Then we were shipped to Honolulu, Hawaii, for another week before finally being sent back to the
Fitzsimmons Army Hospital in Denver, Colorado. I was put
in a ward with some young soldiers who were in pretty bad
shape. Some of them had their arms cut off, some their legs.
It was an awful sight.

The colonel who was in charge of our fourth floor was
a very military man, a disciplinarian, and a pretty tough guy.
Everybody respected him and didn't say too much about him.
One day I was walking down the ward, and I heard some
people arguing. Someone was saying, "I'm going to see my
son whether you like it or not!" There was really loud talk
going on out there. Sure enough, it was my dad. Every time
he would talk, the old colonel would get tough and raise his
voice, too. One of my friends in the ward told me my parents
had come up to the hospital and were looking for me. My
mother was standing out in the hallway, and I ran out there

to hug and kiss her. It had been quite a while since we had seen each other.

We could hear my dad in the colonel's office. Dad was a tough man. When he wanted to say something, he would say it with no beating around the bush. "Colonel, I don't give a damn who in the hell you are or who you represent, but I'm taking my son home for Christmas," he said. "If I have to take him home without clothes, I'm going to do it. Which way do you want it? Do you want me to take him right out like he is or not? I'm giving you a choice. Whichever way, I'm going to take him, and I don't care what you think!"

I thought the old colonel would surely grab him and throw him out the door, but he didn't. Pretty soon, the colonel's receptionist came into the hallway and told me to report to the commissary to get my clothes. They gave me a new complete uniform with extra underclothes, everything I needed. Then I reported to finance, got paid, and was told to report back upstairs to my colonel. Dad was still in there arguing with him. The colonel wanted to give me fifteen days' recuperation time but Dad said, "No, I want thirty days for him." I guess Dad finally out-talked him, because the colonel granted me the thirty-day convalescent leave.

Along with Dad and Mom were my Uncle Jimmy and Aunt Josie. As Dad came out of the hospital, he hugged and kissed me, too, and we went to the car to start back to Alliance. This car they had was a real old one. I remember that. It was wintertime, the middle of December, and really cold. As we started, Dad said, "Mike, I'm going to stop somewhere here and get myself a pint of whiskey."

Dad was a drinking man. At that time, the 1950s, there was a federal law forbidding Indian people to purchase liquor. So even though he liked to drink, Dad had a hard time getting any alcohol. We stopped at a little town somewhere in Colorado, and Dad and I went into the liquor store. He said, "Mike, you try and buy it because I know this guy is going to turn me down." In those days they'd ask for your

ID right away, and if they found out you were an Indian, they wouldn't sell any liquor to you. So I went in.

I had my patches and medals on—the Combat Infantryman Badge, the Korean Service Medal, the Japanese Occupation, the Purple Heart, and others that had been awarded to me in Fitzsimmons Army Hospital. When I walked in this liquor store, the store operator looked at me and asked, "Did you just get back from Korea?" I told him, "Yeah, I'm headed home for Christmas." Of course I had a cast on my arm under my jacket, so I suppose he knew right away that I had come back from combat duty. Without saying anything further he said, "What do you want, kid?" I told him two six-packs of beer and two pints of whiskey. I got my money out, but he said, "No, this is free. This is on the house." At that time, I didn't drink very much, maybe a couple of beers with the guys—that was about it. When we got back to the car, my dad told Uncle Jimmy, Aunt Josie, and Mom what had happened. I thought it was real nice of that guy to do this for us. That was the first time my dad was in a liquor store and was able to get served.

When we got back to Alliance, all of our neighbors, friends, and Emma were at our house. I suppose Dad had told them what time to expect us back. Anyway, that night they were going to give a big dance, an honoring dance for my serving in Korea and coming back home safe. Everybody was so happy to see me, and I them. Mom told me she knew I was shot on Thanksgiving Day. When they were having their Thanksgiving dinner, the man came to the door with the telegram from the War Department saying I was wounded in action in Korea, November 23. She said they received this telegram on November 23. I suppose it could have been the time difference, but I never could really understand it. It just seemed like I'd been to hell and back, which was probably true.

The next night we did have our dance in my mother and father's small house. There must have been fifty or sixty people there. We had an Indian dance, and my dad told me they were going to give me a warrior's name. A medicine man by the name of Sam Kills Crow Indian, who was a very important person in the Indian community in Alliance, was selected to do the honors. Halfway through the Rabbit Dance, everything stopped. Mr. Kills Crow Indian took me to the center of the living room where we were to have our cere- mony. He told everyone I had gone to Korea, fought for my country, and had earned a warrior's name. Then he decided that I would be called Mato Yamni ("Three Bears"). Every- one present was asked if this name was agreeable and if they thought it was good enough to honor me. Everyone decided yes. So I became Mato Yamni for fighting for my country, for being an American soldier, for being an Indian. This was a great, great honor. I felt so proud, so good that I was able to do this and make my Indian community, my mother, fa- ther, brothers, and sisters so proud of me. I forgot about the hardships, all about the freezing nights and days!

About a week later two guys I vaguely knew in Alli- ance and who went into the service with me came around, knocked on the door, and said, "Mark, by golly, we're home, you're home, let's go out and get drunk." I don't think they really understood the significance of Indians' not being al- lowed to have any alcohol, that we couldn't even go into a liquor store, or consume alcohol unless we did it hiding in a back alley some place or in a car. I went along, and we drove around for a bit and drank a couple of beers. Then one of my friends wanted to go down to the American Legion Club. I told them that I couldn't go into that club because no In- dians were allowed in there, but they didn't believe me and just said, "Hell!" I had my uniform on, all my decorations plus the Korean patch. These two guys hadn't even been overseas.

Finally, I went with them. We went up to the American Legion door, and one of the guys pressed the little buzzer. A Mexican bartender peeked out the window. It was one of those one-way windows where he could see us but we couldn't see him. One of my friends was drunk, getting obnoxious and pressing on the buzzer constantly. Well, this Mexican bartender opens the door and sees us three guys—me with my Army uniform with badges, another guy also in Army uniform, and the Navy guy with his uniform on. He looked at us and said, "You two," pointing at my two white friends, "can come in, but this guy," pointing at me, "will have to stay out here. I can't let him come in." So right away I thought to myself, here I am back in Alliance, Nebraska, with this racism thing all over again. It was such a let-down feeling for me after being honored by my people and being treated like a human being the way a man should feel about himself. These guys have the privilege of going into this place, but I don't. There's something awfully wrong about this.

One of my two friends got mad at this Mexican guy and said, "Look, I'm gonna take him in whether you like it or not." I was afraid he'd start something, so I tried to dissuade him by saying, "I know that I can't go in there, and I don't want to dishonor you guys. I'm an Indian, and we're not on the same level." My two friends were really mad, and they wanted to go in and raise hell with the American Legion people. It wasn't their fault that the U.S. government for a long time back had classified Indians as less than human, or that there was this feeling on the part of many white people that Indians were a bunch of dirty, drunk, shiftless people. It was very hard for me to understand, but I knew it, and I'd had to live with it all my life.

Later, after I got discharged and came back to Alliance, the Veterans of Foreign Wars, Disabled American Veterans, and American Legion Associations all contacted me and wanted me to join. I told them, "No, I would rather not," as I knew I couldn't go into their building. One guy finally talked me into joining the Disabled American Veterans, so I did. They held their meetings in this same Legion club. I told the commander about not being able to attend meetings there because of having to walk through a room where liquor was served. He told me not to worry but to join, and "we'll get you to the meetings."

One night I came late to a meeting, and this same Mexican bartender came to the door and wouldn't let me in or even tell the commander that I was there. So I missed the meeting, and I was furious. The next day I explained to the commander what had happened and told him I was going to quit. After that, I just kept away from military organizations altogether even though today they still try to get me to join them.

To get back to 1950, I stayed home for just thirty days on convalescent leave, enjoying my family and friends. I still had to report back to the hospital, but I wasn't hurt bad enough to get a medical discharge. After going back to Fitzsimmons Army Hospital for another thirty days' stay, my arm and leg healed. They gave me another fifteen-day leave before I was sent to Camp Aturbury, Indiana, about thirty miles out of Indianapolis. I was kind of scared. It was the first time I'd ever heard of it. I found out that Camp Aturbury was the National Guard outfit out of Pennsylvania—the Twenty-eighth Division—and I was assigned to that outfit. There were a lot of really young guys—all of my company came from Erie, Pennsylvania. They were real nice men.

I remember the first day reporting to Company B, to Captain Ford. I thought the reason I was put in this company was to help train the troops. Of course, at that time, I was private first class, which wasn't a very high rank in the Army. The next morning when I woke up and looked on the bulletin board, there was PFC Monroe assigned to work on garbage detail. It kind of seemed odd to me that after serving in Korea and being decorated with many ribbons, I would end up in a National Guard company that had never been away from home and work all day hauling trash and garbage.

That evening about five o'clock when we got through

working, Captain Ford came over to me and apologized. "Private Monroe," he said, "I am very sorry. I just received your orders at noon. I did not know that you had served in Korea, and I'm sorry that I put you on this garbage detail. You are here strictly to help train the troops." I said, "I've done this before, and it doesn't make any difference to me." Captain Ford was very apologetic and asked me what I wanted to do. So I told him I was first gunner on an 81-milli-meter mortar and was in the head ordnance company. "I'm going to put you in charge of the squad," Captain Ford said, "and I want you to teach them everything you learned in Korea."

When we'd go out on training exercises, I would teach them how to operate the gun fast, correctly, and efficiently. I did this about three months, and was the teacher for a whole company of a hundred and six men. When their training was completed, the National Guard began to train other troops who were drafted into the Army.

One of the things that happened to me while stationed at Camp Aturbury was that nights after six, when all work was done, I'd go to the PX in my uniform, which, of course, was decorated with a lot of ribbons and medals. Some of the new guys coming in about my age who had probably been in the Army only two to three months were really amazed at the fact that I had been in Korea and come back alive. Just for being in the PX wearing all these medals, the guys would all buy me beer and candy. I was some kind of a hero to them. It made me feel real good.

Captain Ford was a real nice guy and didn't care too much about Army protocol; usually a captain doesn't talk much with a PFC or corporal. But one day Captain Ford asked me what I'd like to do next, now that I had helped train the troops and there was nothing more to do. I told him I liked to work in the kitchen so he said okay. He mentioned that I had been there about four months and asked me if I wanted to go on a furlough. "No," I told him, "I'd rather stay another three months. My parents are very poor, and I can't afford to go home." So the captain said he'd think about this a little bit and see what he could do.

Well, I started working in the kitchen as a KP pusher. That was what they called it at that time. My job was to show the KPs who came on duty what to do and make sure they did it. It was a good solid job supervising them. KP means "kitchen police." These young recruits who worked in the kitchen had to keep it clean, wash dishes, wash up the dining room and kitchen. I was kind of rough on them, and right away some of the young guys started calling me "Whip."

I had been working in the kitchen about a week when Captain Ford called me into his office and said, "I always like to see my people go home every three to four months. You've been away from home over four months, and I'd like to see you take a furlough." I explained to him that I sent almost half of my pay home to my mother, forty-five or forty-six dollars a month, and kept the other fifty dollars to live on. "Well," said Captain Ford, "I'll tell you what we did. All the sergeants in the company, many of the company men, and I have all pitched in and made donations so that we are sending you home on a furlough. How do you like that?" I told him I couldn't believe it that they would send me home, pay my train fare and everything. I was kind of shocked, but there was no way I could turn Captain Ford down. I got the money, my fifteen-day furlough, and was told to leave in the morning. That evening, I called my mother up at home and told her the good news. I was so thankful after coming back to Camp Aturbury that I thanked the captain and even wrote him a thank-you note.

While I was working in the kitchen, our mess sergeant, Sergeant Lucas, took an interest in me and started to teach me how to cook. He said after I got out of the Army I'd have a vocation. So I went to the cook and bakery school for about nine weeks right there at Camp Aturbury. I learned the basics of cooking meat, vegetables, fish, and so on. After I got out of that school, I came back to the company area and began cooking in the kitchen as second cook.

During the latter part of September 1951, we learned that the Twenty-eighth Division was going to be shipped to Germany, to be stationed there until after the war. Captain Ford asked me if I would like to come along. I told him I would. It meant reenlisting for a couple of years so I had to call my parents and tell them what I wanted to do. They were very negative about it. They wanted me to come home when my discharge was due; they felt I'd done enough in the Army. My parents were very possessive, and I was still probably a child listening to their orders and directives. I reported back to Captain Ford. Evidently my mother had written him and thanked him for sending me back on furlough. Now she wrote and told him she did not want me to go to Germany. Captain Ford understood. He kind of agreed with her because I had been to Korea in the Asiatic theater, and he decided to go along with her wishes. I had just begun to make it in the Army, and it made me feel so darn bad to be leaving. I liked the men in our company, and there was a lot of respect between us, the officers and the noncommissioned officers as well.

The day came when I was supposed to be transferred to another regiment in Camp Aturbury, a holding company for soldiers to be discharged. Captain Ford called me into his office where he had a sheet all ready and my clothes packed; he shook my hand and said, "Nice having you." The jeep took me to the far end of the camp. It was a pretty good-sized base, maybe five to six miles away. I went to this holding company the latter part of September and was due to be discharged November 21 or 22.

When I arrived, Colonel Getman was the company commander. When he looked at my records and found out I'd been in Korea and had a cook MOS since coming to Camp Aturbury, he was happy. He asked me if I could take charge of the kitchen. I said, "You bet." I could cook a complete meal for breakfast, dinner, and supper and got to the point where I was pretty good at it. Colonel Getman immediately gave me five KPs and a cook's helper from the National Guard outfit. We set to work cleaning out the kitchen, which was dusty and dirty and hadn't been opened in six or seven months. I really liked my job as supervisor of the kitchen.

Finally we got about one hundred and twenty men in our holding company. A lot of the guys were ready for discharge and didn't want to go overseas. I asked Colonel Getman for another shift of cooks, cook's helpers, and KPs so I would only work five days a week and another cook would work weekends. It began to look like I'd never get discharged, as Colonel Getman liked my cooking so well and good cooks were hard to get. But on November 25, 1951, he called me into his office and asked me if I'd like to reenlist for three more years. I told him no. So he asked me who was my best helper over there to train. Then we went into the process of getting me discharged, which took a week.

The Korean War was an important part of my life, but not one that I'm too proud of. I didn't know where that country was or what we were fighting for in Korea. I killed a lot of people and saw the damage our guns did to some of the villages we raided. I've never wanted to talk about it very much. Lots of times I hear guys bragging about what they'd done overseas, how many people they'd killed, and how many days of combat they'd served. Usually I'll just sit around and listen, feeling it's probably good for them to talk about it. The only thing I'm proud of is that I enlisted, went where I was told to go, followed orders, and did everything a U.S. soldier should do to represent his country well.

However, my time at Camp Aturbury as a member of the Twenty-eighth Division was something I'll never forget. It was the only time that I felt accepted and liked as a human being. These men from Erie, Pennsylvania, were a good bunch: Captain Ford, Lieutenant Jankowski, who was an officer but acted like a friend, and Corporal Parker, who worked in the kitchen with me and was one of the finest gentlemen I have ever met. Also there was Sergeant "Stoosh" Kenny and Corporal Bill Frombaugh. These guys went out of their way to teach me the cooking trade. I think it was the first time that they had ever met an American Indian—and one who had been in the war and had come back! They were all young guys, maybe a year or two older than I was.

Corporal Grau was a new guy in our company, but I'll always remember him, too. He was a German and had been in the German army before he came to the United States; when he came to New York, he was drafted into our army and wound up at Camp Aturbury. Of course, he'd never met an Indian before, so he asked me a lot of questions. I, in turn, was kind of amazed that he had been in the German army in World War II. So we had long conversations about my being Indian and his being German. He told me that when he was in the German army, the American soldier was portrayed as a killer, a beast who wouldn't take any prisoners. Consequently, all the German soldiers were deathly afraid of us Americans. Over here, the United States portrayed the German and Japanese armies as people who were ruthless and killed everything in sight. I remembered this from when I was younger, through the movies and newspapers. I think the political thing was to scare the heck out of both sides. Corporal Grau and I became very good friends. While he was at Camp Aturbury, he met and married an Irish girl from Erie, Pennsylvania. I never saw him again after I was discharged, for he was one of the guys who went to Germany with the Twenty-eighth Division.

My time at Camp Aturbury was the best experience of my young life away from Alliance. These people went completely out of their way to help me, encourage me, and to humanize me. I really enjoyed it, and it gave me a good feeling. Although I was crippled in my left arm, could only use my thumb and first finger to work with, I learned a new vocation.

When I got discharged and came back to Alliance, I knew as soon as I got off the train that we were back into the old hierarchy again. Even though my parents, brothers, sisters, and girlfriend Emma were all there at the train station to meet me, I couldn't help feeling I'm back to the old rut of living in a racist town with nothing in sight jobwise. God, I wish I could have gone to Germany with the Twenty-eighth Division! Here was my chance to become a career soldier, but it didn't work out as my parents asked me to come home. They were very possessive of me, and I couldn't understand it at the time, but years later when I had children of my own, I did.

The day after I arrived back in Alliance, I went to the VA service officer, who made arrangements for me to go to Cheyenne, Wyoming. After questioning me, they awarded me a 30 percent disability with combat pay as well as back pay. About six months later I received my veteran's compensation and forty-five dollars a month, which at that time was a lot of money. A guy could pay his rent, utility bills, and get a little food with that. But my disability hindered my working in heavy construction because my left hand was of no use to me in that kind of work. Well, I had to do something like I did in the Army, so I started looking around.

C·H·A·P·T·E·R IV

FIRST BAKER
A Trade and a Family

My girlfriend, Emma, waited for me while I was in the Army, and we were married March 29, 1952. I had met her sometime in 1946, when she was only fourteen years old, and I was a year and a half older. Her parents and my parents knew each other, I think, even when they lived in South Dakota. I used to go to the Lone Wolfs' house and visit with them, and there I met Emma. You would call us childhood sweethearts.

In the 1940s I had an old 1929 Model A car that I would pick her up in. We went to the theater or to a show. At that time there were no taverns, but she didn't drink and I didn't either. The reason I was so attracted to Emma at first was because she was the most beautiful woman I had ever seen, met, or talked to. She had class even when she was young. She dressed clean at all times and just acted like a lady. I don't think there were very many times in our married life that I ever heard her cuss. All during the time we were going together, I knew that I was falling madly in love with Emma. I think she was with me, too.

When we were going steady, it was a real good clean type of relationship. I knew that Emma's mother and father liked me very much. My parents loved Emma like one of their own children. It was like we were planned for marriage. Emma was the only girl that I had ever known, and to this day, now that she's gone, I am still suffering from being so close to her. Emma was the kind of person who was very dedicated. While we were going together and even more so after our marriage, she dedicated her life to me. I could never say anything bad about her. To me she was a perfect

woman—one out of a million. I always wondered why a
beautiful person like Emma would ever fall in love with an
ugly guy like me. Maybe that's the reason why I was so possessive of her. I always remember, ever since I met Emma, if
she ever did or said anything wrong, she always told me. I
myself would try to be as open with her, but there were a lot
of things I didn't tell her.

When Emma and I decided to get married, money was
pretty scarce. Both of our families were very poor. They were
barely surviving, barely eating—just barely making their way.
We decided to get married by a justice of the peace even
though Emma was a very good Catholic and liked to go to
church. We knew that later on in our marriage we would get
married in the church, which we did. At the time, it was
more important to be together, and because of the economic
situation, we couldn't afford anything else. Emma's parents
and my parents knew that we were going to get married, and
they were very happy about it. My mother and father were
our best man and best woman. We had no large ceremony or
give-away. Now that I am a little bit better off financially, I
kind of wish that we could relive those days because I would
have done anything for Emma.

When we first got married, we moved into this apartment in Chimneytown, which is now Good Samaritan Vil-
lage. At first, we were even chaperoned by my brother-in-law
George Lone Wolf, and his wife, Myrtle, who moved in with
us right away. They had their own bedroom, and we had
ours. I liked George and Myrtle very much. They were real
good people. George sometimes still kids me that he didn't
trust me with his sister, so that's why he moved in with us on
our wedding night. That's how close our family is. I felt a
sense of security living with them, that I would be able to do
anything that I tried to do.

I was getting used to being in Alliance again and missing the Army when I got a job in a construction outfit pushing cement in a wheelbarrow. I had a hard time doing it

because I could barely hold the wheelbarrow handle with my thumb and first finger. At the time I was working with my brother-in-law. He'd watch me as I got a hold of this old wheelbarrow, and the man would fill it clear full of cement; I'd try to lift it up, but my left arm would slip and the cement would go all over the ground. George was always poking fun at me for that. I had a hard time adjusting to civilian life. In the Army I was awarded such soft jobs and given everything I could do. When I came out here, I had to do this heavy work, but I just kept trying anyway.

Shortly after Emma and I were married, I received all my back compensation and some combat pay. This amounted to a couple of thousand bucks. So I felt very good and started looking for better work. The VA office wanted to send me for training, so I started working as a body and fender man at one of our local garages. My job was to learn how to fix dented fenders and paint them. But the one thing we forgot, the VA office and I, was that my left hand was crippled and I could not do that kind of work, so I learned to be a painter instead. I learned how to paint cars, tractors, and things like that real well. Fact is, my boss, whose name was Robertson, made arrangements with another garage that handled tractors, combines, and implements. They would bring their farm machinery into his shop, and I would paint them at a reduction in price. That way I made some good money.

As a year went by, I was under the constant watch or care of the VA people, who would come in and check to see how I was doing and adapting to the painting job. They finally decided that this was not the vocation they wanted to keep me in and spend thousands of bucks teaching me how to do, when I couldn't do it according to their specifications because of my physical impairment. After about a year I was taken off the painting job by the VA, and they said they would look for something that I would be better qualified for. Mr. Robertson, however, told me he would go ahead and pay me a regular wage if I'd continue working for him, but I figured, well, I better do what the VA suggests and get some kind of training where I can make a good living for myself in my later years.

Our first daughter, Connie, was born December 23, 1952. We had a real happy married life. We weren't living with our parents like other Indian children. We had an apartment in Chimneytown and were very proud of that fact. I bought us a new Studebaker. It wasn't a brand-new one, but a 1950 model that Mr. Robertson gave me a good deal on. Emma and I were the first Indian people in Alliance to own a practically new car, and it sure was something to feel good about.

During this time I was drinking, not heavily, but on weekends whenever I could get it. If someone offered me a drink, I took it. While in the Army I didn't drink much— maybe I'd go out to the PX once in a while, have three or four beers, come back to the barracks, and let it go at that. It was never a problem for me. But by the third year of our marriage, I noticed that I was beginning to drink more than normal. I always managed to keep my job and do good work. That was one of the things I required of myself. I think I must have known I was beginning to drink too much. Why in the world I didn't quit then, I don't know.

A month or two before our first son, Terry, was born on May 17, 1954, I started working in Schad's Bakery in Alliance. The VA found out I had learned to be a cook in the Army, and they wanted to train me to become a baker for a three-year period. I said, "My real vocation is to cook, but if it is anything to do with baking, I think I'll adapt to it." They started me baking in early 1953, first as a cleanup man and helping with whatever the first and second bakers would do. One of the jobs was to grease all the pans and make sure all the flour and sugar barrels were filled up. Whenever the baker would empty bread out of the oven, I picked the bread up and put it on the shelves. I thought I'd learn everything from the ground up. In the mornings, from four to five o'clock, I'd have to take this scraper and scrape the entire floor completely clean of grease, flour, and dirt. The man I worked for was very clean. I would do this and clean the oven and all the mixers for making donuts. They had an automatic donut machine, so all I had to do was to stir the mix (it came already mixed), add water, and make the donuts.

Our second son, Daryl, was born May 29, 1955, at home. My mother-in-law, Jenny Lone Wolf, was the midwife. Jenny was our spiritual woman so she did deliver a lot of Indian babies in Alliance, and a lot of people were dependent upon her. Daryl was real healthy as a baby and still is.

When I first started working in the bakery, I think it was hard for Emma to get used to me working nights. We weren't ever apart, and I felt real bad leaving my wife at home with three little ones and working for ten to twelve hours. Well, I learned everything about the bakery business, from baking the goods to selling them, to retailing, ordering, and purchasing supplies. It was a very good trade for me. I have always considered myself a journeyman baker, and, if my health was good now, I could go anywhere in the United States and be the first baker in a bakery. But I think that is where I started to drink heavily and became an alcoholic.

During my training days at Schad's Bakery I worked with the head baker, Red Hawley, and the baker's helper, Ted, who was the boss's son. Ted and I were about the same age, and he was learning the bakery trade, too, but his father owned the bakery so he got the better job. I got along pretty good with both Red and Ted. They did not have any racial thoughts and were more concerned about how much work a man could do and the kind of work he did. I was always proud that I could handle the work, do as I was told, and learn the trade.

After about two years of training, Red Hawley quit, and so did Ted. One night the boss came up to me and asked if I wanted to be the head baker. He would teach me for a couple of weeks, and then I could go ahead and run the shop.

I told him I would. For about two weeks Mr. Schadwinkel came in and taught me the finer aspects of baking. Of course, in the couple of years that I had worked there I had already learned a lot. When both bakers quit and I took over, I was very nervous and very scared because the head baker's role in the bakery is a very important one. He has to make a lot of decisions and put out real fine goods to hold his job. I think I had more to prove as an American Indian, especially in Alliance.

I had all these things going against me, but I started work as the head baker, and I guess I did a real good job. There were a lot of compliments from Mr. Schadwinkel and his sister, Erna, about how well I was doing and the time I put in trying to learn. Whenever the VA man would come in to inspect my work, the Schadwinkels always put in a good word for me. I really felt good about it. There was another man by the name of Mike Banjof who worked at the Delite Bakery across the street. Mike took a liking to me, and whenever I had a problem, I would call him and ask him what I had done wrong or what I could have done to make a better loaf of bread or buns. He showed me.

After about a year as first baker and having to prove I could do just as good or better a job than a white baker could, I heard through the grapevine from some of my friends that many of the people in Alliance did not like the fact that the Schadwinkels had an Indian baker they were grooming to take over the first baker's job. I never heard even once Mr. Schadwinkel, his wife, or his sister complain about the fact I was an Indian. The only thing that they looked for from me was to be on the job, to do good work, and put out good products. I seemed to be doing this. I talked with Mr. Schadwinkel quite a few times. He always complimented me on what I was doing and never brought up the fact that I was an Indian. The Schadwinkel family was one of the most prominent families in Alliance. They were what Mr. Schadwinkel himself called "high German." They were the kind of people that I was always afraid of because I felt maybe they might be discriminatory toward Indian people. Well, after I met them and started working for them, I knew they were the kind of people who looked at you as a person, at your productivity, not the color of your skin.

So I was feeling real good in the bakery, and the more I worked, the more self-confidence I had. I did a really good job. I only regret that when I worked there, I began to drink too much. Mr. Schadwinkel didn't seem to mind as long as everything was done properly, looked good, and tasted good. He was an alcoholic himself. Someone told me that he drank a quart of whiskey plus a case or couple of cases of beer a day. He spent all of his waking hours at the Elks Club. I never paid much attention to this because he was a very good man and very understanding.

The longer I worked at the bakery, the more I was drinking and liking it too much. This was also affecting my family. I think during my baking years in the 1950s, $100 a week was one of the top wages for electricians, plumbers, and carpenters. I started working at the bakery for $75 a week and was also getting $75 a week from the government. So I would get $150 a week, and this put me in a higher salary bracket than even our first baker.

About ten years later, when I was having drinking problems, I mentioned to Emma that if we had saved our money when I was baking, we would have had a lot put aside. But I drank most of it up. In 1954, when President Eisenhower signed the bill making liquor legally available for Indian people, I met a lot of retail liquor salesmen, and they knew I liked to drink, so I opened a couple of accounts at some of the local liquor stores. One night I went to pay my liquor bill for one week. The man put down the bill, and I owed $64 for that one week alone for beer, whiskey, and all I was drinking that day. This also accounted for Emma and my friends, who would drink on weekends. Emma and I were kind of the social leaders in our Indian community at that time because of the high salary I was making and the good home we maintained. We always had a lot of bread, rolls, cakes, and just about everything that the bakery made. Mr. Schadwinkel told me that we could have whatever we needed. So every evening before I'd go to work, Emma's mom and dad or some of my family would come over and they'd eat whatever we had. We were the first Indian family in Alliance to have a TV, and that also made us popular because many of our friends would come over and watch TV in the evening. Emma and I were very happy. I was spending the money, though, as fast as we could get it. When I remember back, I think, my God, whenever a man and his friends would drink up half of his salary a week, there has to be something wrong.

When Red Hawley quit, Mr. Schadwinkel said, "Mick, you are going to have to get someone to assist you, and you're going to have to teach this man what you know so he can be your helper." As soon as he said that to me, I figured I was in the same situation as Mr. Hawley was when he hired me. He had to teach two guys the trade, because Ted and I had both just got out of the Army, and we were learning. I always kind of felt sorry for Red because he had two guys to teach; now I was in the same position. I had to teach a baker's helper and learn myself at the same time. But I got to the point where I knew very well what to do; it was just a matter of doing it, and getting enough help.

I hired my sister's husband, whose name was Leonard Bordeaux. In the evenings when we'd go in at six-thirty, I'd start figuring out basically what amount of doughs we would need for a hundred and fifty loaves of bread and a hundred dozen rolls, as each item took a different type of dough. I still had to teach Leonard how to grease the pans and help mix the dough. His job was to carry the flour into the compartment where it was dumped and then take it to the mixer. Then we hired another man to scrape the floors, sweep, and clean, and I also had to teach him.

It was rough. For about a year the hardest part of my whole life was just teaching these two men how to do what I had already learned. Leonard seemed to learn very well, but he was hot-tempered, and he couldn't get along with me. I could get along with him well enough, but one night he just quit. All the time that I had spent teaching him, probably two years, just went down the drain. So Shorty Lance and I ran the bakery. He was a very good helper, but he didn't know how to work at the table where all the cutting and kneading of the dough was done, as he hadn't had that kind of experience.

Shorty, my helper at the bakery, was almost a part of our family. Shorty's name was Lawrence Lance. He had come to our family about the latter part of 1952. My dad had the trash-hauling contract for the city of Alliance, and he had two trucks. What I would do on weekends, or whenever I was off, was help him pick up trash down the alleys, load it into the truck, and take it out to the dump. One day Dad and I were unloading our trash, and sitting out there in the middle of the dump was this hobo. We went over and we started talking to him. Shorty was a pretty nice fellow. He was a very short guy, dark and dark-haired; he kind of looked like an Indian, but you could tell he was a white man. After he and Dad had been talking a while, Shorty jumped in the truck, and we brought him on home.

Dad had an old shack behind his house, and Shorty stayed there. He and Dad always got along very well. Shorty started helping Dad on the truck and also doing yard work around the house. He became a very important member of our family and stayed with us about twenty-six years. I always remember my dad proudly saying to other people at that time that he was the only Indian in Alliance who had a built-in bootlegger! Whenever Dad wanted a jug of wine, beer, or whiskey, Shorty would buy it for him free of charge. At that time, whenever Indian people wanted a drink, well, they'd have to pay the bootlegger double.

We had a shower in the bakery that you could use when you went to work and when you got off. It was very convenient, and you could keep very clean. Shorty was the third man at the bakery. The third man is the one that does all the cleaning, scraping floors, and cleaning pans. That's the job I'd started with. Shorty stayed there with us in the bakery for at least twenty years, even after I fired myself. In the long run, I think Mr. Schadwinkel was very happy with some of the things I did at the bakery and some of the people that I taught. Everything that I did proved to be positive.

It was really a lot of fun working with Shorty. One time, he had a really hard time keeping shoes on. He was always wearing great big shoes that he'd find at the dump, but Al didn't like that. He told Shorty he'd have to get some better-looking shoes. So Shorty told him, "Al, I can't find shoes to fit me." Al told him to take off his shoes, and I swear that he must have worn a size eight or nine E. Al looked at his feet and said he was going to order a pair of specially made shoes from some shoe manufacturing company in Boston, Massachusetts. One night Al came back to the bakery and gave Shorty the craziest pair of shoes I've ever seen in my life. They looked like boxes and were just as wide as they were long. Shorty was really happy. He put them on, and the shoes did seem to fit him. Old Al must have paid three or four times as much as ten dollars for those shoes.

But that night, I saw Shorty limping around. The next night he came to work, and Al was there. As Shorty came into the bakery with his new shoes on, I saw that Shorty had sliced the shoes where his little toes go because they were too tight. I said, "Oh God, if old Al sees this, he's going to really raise a lot of hell." Al came in, and when he looked at those new shoes that Shorty had cut, he was so disgusted that he shook his head and walked out.

All the Indian people liked Shorty, and they liked to drink with him because he would buy all the drinks. He made pretty good money at the bakery. By Saturday night, of course, he would be broke. I don't think Shorty ever missed a night in the twenty years he worked in the bakery. He was a hard worker, and I was kind of proud that I had introduced him to the bakery trade, because he was good at it. He never did get any advancement, just stayed at that same level. He was the third man at the bakery, the cleanup man, and he liked that.

Shorty stayed with us and just became a member of our family; he was very close to all of us until 1976, when he went back to Pittsburgh, Pennsylvania. Someone told me later on that he died, but I've never heard a word about him, and it sometimes makes me feel lonesome that I don't know what really happened to him.

Shorty and I ran the bakery for probably another six months without a third man, but we managed to do it. I was very proud that after going in as a baker's apprentice, I worked myself up to the point where I could teach other people this trade. When our VA contact man came in and found out that I was given the head baker's position, well, he was very happy and wrote on my report that I was training other people for this position as a baker. Of course, I never would have been able to do it without Mr. Schadwinkel's good help, understanding, and teaching. Now that I think back on those days, Mr. Schadwinkel played a very important part in my life. He gave me dignity and pride. He gave me everything that it takes to make a person feel like a man.

I always remember one thing about Mr. Schadwinkel. He was a kind of quiet, businesslike type of guy. Whenever he was working on the table, he spent a lot of time drinking out of a glass that was half full of whiskey and half full of beer. He never stopped working, just long enough to take a drink, and he'd mumble a few words. If you were doing something wrong, he would just tell you, and that was it. He was a very good boss. I think that if he hadn't drunk so

much, he would probably have been a great man. He taught
well and did his job well. I highly respected him and didn't
give a damn whether he drank or not.

After we'd get done baking around four or five o'clock
in the morning, Mike Banjof, who ran the bakery across the
street, would come over and sit around the bakery drinking
with us. If I stayed, I would drink with them and play cards.
Even though I was treated like a fellow human being, lots of
times I would go home because I didn't want to start drinking. I was still fighting that part of me that liked alcohol too
much. I knew I shouldn't be doing it, but I would end up
doing it anyway.

After Leonard quit and Shorty and I had worked the
night shift for quite a while, Al asked me if I could find
somebody to be my helper. I said I would try one more time,
and I asked my brother Bill, who was four years younger
than I, if he wanted to learn the bakery trade. I said we'd
start him out with $75 a week. So Bill came to work one
night, and I started teaching him what I knew about the bakery trade. Even though the bakery business is hard manual
type of labor, you're always busy from the minute you go in
to work until the time you walk out. Bill is a very intelligent
person, but I knew about a week after he started there that
he wasn't used to this kind of labor. It was a very fast type
of work, and we never had any regular hours like an eight-
hour or nine-hour shift. We worked according to the orders
we were given. If we could work fast enough, maybe we
could get done in six hours, or, if we had a larger order,
maybe it would take us eight hours. It just depended on how
we mixed the doughs, how they fermented, and how we cut
it up to make the bread, rolls, and buns. It was mostly up to
the bakers themselves how long the shift would last. I did for
Bill what Mr. Schadwinkel had done for me, and I offered
him a lot of compliments and made him feel like a human
being. He gained confidence even though he made some mis-
takes and was tired at times.

Bill and I had started school in Alliance together. He grew up with the impression that Alliance was a very racist town and, if you were an Indian, you could not get ahead. I knew Bill had the same problem I had. I think it was a little more comfortable for him because his brother was the head baker. Bill did a real good job. Fact is that when I left the bakery, he became the head baker, and I think the Schadwinkel people liked the fact that I taught Bill. He is now working in Omaha, Nebraska, in one of the Nabisco cracker companies as a baker. He has continued in the baking trade and is making a good living. Due to family problems, I haven't seen him since our father's death in 1981, but I understand he is doing well.

Back then, I fell into the same pattern Mr. Hawley and Mr. Schadwinkel had—drinking while working—and Bill did also. It's kind of a bad memory for me, as I think I may have influenced my brother in the wrong way. When he first came to the bakery to work, he only drank a few beers on weekends. When he worked with me, he started drinking a lot more. It really concerned me. Bill learned the trade the same way I did, and having him working with me seemed to take some of the pressure off of me. I never took a day or a night off no matter how drunk or tired I got. I'd have to be there because I was the only guy other than Mr. Schadwinkel who knew how to do it.

During the time Bill, Shorty, and I were working till around two or three in the morning, we would be telling ghost stories to pass time and getting ourselves spooky. Indian people believe in ghosts, you know, in a kind of a beautiful way. We are more sensitive to them and believe more in the spiritual world than do non-Indian people. One Monday night in 1956, after Emma's brother, Tommy, had gotten beaten up one Saturday night and was in the hospital where he was expected to die, we were working late and talking as usual. I was really worried about Tommy. Emma and I had gone up to the hospital Sunday afternoon, but he was still in

a coma. Now, early Monday morning while we were all
working, all of a sudden we heard a man scream. It was so
plain that I thought someone had walked in the bakery's
back door and had yelled. We all heard it, and each one of us
got really frightened.

About two or three minutes later the phone rang, and
it was Emma, who was at the hospital. She said that Tommy
had just died. When I told Shorty and Bill what had happened, we all figured we heard Tommy yell at the time that
he died.

I think the spookiness of night work affected some of
the people who came in to work for us later on. Sometimes
when we'd have a real big order, I'd hire one of Emma's
nephews to help clean up for us so Shorty could be available
to help bake and ice the rolls. One night I had one of her
nephews come in, and he was a very nervous guy. I don't
think he was much older than I was, but he believed in
ghosts, and he didn't like to work at night. When he came
into the bakery, I told him to go downstairs and put on a
white uniform, clean up, and go to work.

So he went downstairs, but, by golly, about two minutes later, he ran up the stairs, his face as white as a sheet. I
asked him what was the matter, and he wouldn't tell me.
Something had scared him down there in the basement. He
started to work, but while he was sweeping the floor and
cleaning up, he kept looking around. He made every one of
us spooky. Then he went home and told everybody else that
the bakery was haunted, and he didn't want to go there any
more.

Sometimes when I sit around and think about some of
the things that happened, I wonder whether we were all over-
reacting, or if those things did really happen. Maybe they
gave me more reason to drink.

During the time that I took over the head baker's job,
one thing I had to do was come in about three o'clock in the

afternoon and mix a bread sponge. This consisted of a few ounces of salt, flour, and water, which helped the dough to ferment. Then I came back and started at six-thirty in the evening, and if I got off at four o'clock in the morning, regardless of what I was doing, I'd have to be in the bakery again at three o'clock the next afternoon to mix this sponge. It reminded me of the Army, where you had to do what they told you to do. I loved the Army, but I didn't like the regimentation. I really hated that aspect of the bakery business and thought, here I am back in the same regimented pattern, and I've got to be here. If I'm not, there's no bread, rolls, or buns the next day. It may have been another reason why I started to drink so much.

But I think that somewhere deep in my mind, I was also fighting the fact that I did not want to become an alcoholic. (Of course, in those days I did not know what it meant to be an alcoholic; terms like that came later in my life.) I was also concerned about my brother Bill, following my pattern as he did. But now that I know more about alcoholism, I realize Bill was not an alcoholic, because he could drink and he could stop.

I did sometimes wonder how Emma could put up with me working at the bakery six nights a week. Sometimes I'd start at six-thirty in the evening and work until eleven o'clock the next day. Emma was home alone with the children, but she never complained. She was just a good wife. She understood my trade and that it was the kind of life that we would lead. It was a good life; it offered my family and me opportunities that we had never had before. But I just did things wrong and drank up half my earnings.

Emma drank with me, too, but she was never an alcoholic. She could quit drinking, but I couldn't at that point. Sometimes when I'd wake up in the afternoon, I'd need a beer. I was really worried. Whenever I woke up after I'd been drunk, well, I'd need another drink to straighten out. I some-

times wondered whether the alcohol and me being worried
about it was why I just kind of walked out of the bakery
trade.

As I look back, I don't think it was Mr. Schadwinkel
or his sister or his wife who fired me or laid me off in 1964.
One night I went in, feeling very bad, and I more or less tried
to pick a fight. I think I laid myself off. Probably Mr. Schadwinkel and his family were very happy that Bill was there to
take over. I don't really know what happened to me. I was
making a lot of money and was living very well. Our family
was happy, we were raising our children, and we had moved
to a good home in town. I reached the kind of middle-class
mentality where you think everything is going good for you. I
had come to that point, but I just walked out.

Emma and I continued to raise our family. After Connie, Terry, and Daryl were born, we had a little girl, Donna
Lee, who was stillborn. In 1956 Emma was diagnosed as having diabetes, which she contracted somewhere along the way.
On September 22, 1958, Kandi was born at home, and
Emma's mother, Mrs. Lone Wolf, attended her. I remember
taking Kandi in my arms and saying, "Oh, she's the sweetest
little girl you ever want to see." Right then and there, I gave
her the nickname Kandi, but her real name was Amy Angela
Monroe. We had four more stillborn babies, in 1962, 1963,
and 1964, and the last one six years later in 1970.

Emma became pregnant again, and this time she went
to Pine Ridge Hospital, where another of our babies was stillborn. I was so broke at the time that I had my brother-in-
law, Floyd Leistritz, take me up there. In 1964 I was drinking
so heavily that I didn't have a cent on me. All of it was being
spent on alcohol, and I was out of work at the time because
of my drinking problem. I had no way to bring the baby
back or bury him in Alliance. I told the doctor about our situation, and he said, "Well, go out to the Holy Rosary (that's
the Red Cloud Indian School now), and ask the priest there if

you can bury the baby in their graveyard." So I did go out there with my brother-in-law.

Some of the things I started thinking about then helped me, in the end, become the sober man I am today. But at the time it made me feel so bad that I didn't have money enough to buy a little flower or baby coffin. I felt like a complete pauper and bum. I'd been drinking that morning with Floyd, who had bought some beer. Even though I was a little drunk, I was thinking about these things, and I was so ashamed. I had a shovel with me, and I was able to go to the top of the hill and dig my baby's grave. After preparing the grave, we drove back to the hospital, where the baby's body was given to us. Then I buried the baby myself.

C·H·A·P·T·E·R V

AN ALCOHOLIC
Losing Everything

In the summer of 1964 and into 1965, after I left my full-time job at Schad's Bakery, I began to stay home, working odd jobs in town. Once in a while I'd be called into the Delite Bakery and to Schad's on a part-time basis—whenever one of the bakers would get sick. Sometimes I'd work at the stockyards on Wednesdays and sometimes on a farm part time, but I was drinking steadily all this time. When I was working in the bakery, I drank nothing but whiskey and beer. I always seemed to be able to sober up and get up, work, and do whatever needed to be done the next morning. But when I was working at the stockyards, I was there with a bunch of Indian winos from here in town who constantly drank wine. I told myself I wouldn't drink the wine, but I knew that resisting it was kind of a lost cause, and that I was going to do it anyway. Something within me kept fighting against it, though; I suppose I saw too many guys drinking wine and how it affected their lives and what it did to them.

One day in 1965 when I was working at the stockyards, I brought three of my friends home with me, and they were drinking wine. As soon as Emma saw us, she said, "Mick, please don't drink." Well, I left those guys, but that afternoon when we were working, one of them went up town and got a quart. The kind of work we were doing was chasing cattle and horses from pen to pen. Nobody was watching us, so we could practically do whatever we wanted to. Anyway, that afternoon, I drank wine, and when I got home from work I was drunk. I kept lying to Emma that I had not been drinking, but she knew I had. She became very concerned, and I knew I shouldn't have done it.

At that time Emma was pregnant with Hope. I didn't want to hurt her in any way as I knew she had a heck of a time in her pregnancy, especially with her sugar diabetes and all. But after I started drinking the wine, I really liked it. I noticed that when I drank wine, the next morning when I woke up, God, I'd be sick. Whiskey and beer never did affect me that way. Whenever I could, I would sneak out and get another drink. Every time I did it, Emma would know. There was no sense trying to hide it from her. Women's intuition, I guess.

I don't think at this time that I was completely hooked on wine; I could wake up the next morning and do whatever my job was, if I had one. I think at that time I was drawing about eighty dollars a month compensation from the Army.

In 1965 Emma went to the Pine Ridge Hospital in labor, but there were problems, and on the first of August they sent her to Winnebago, Nebraska, approximately four hundred miles away. I stayed home and watched the children. As soon as Emma left, I started drinking wine heavily; I was becoming a wino I suppose. Even so, I was watching my children and doing a good job of it, and I was always proud that I was able to do that.

I went to Winnebago and stayed with Emma for about two days and three nights. I ran into some Winnebago guys there and drank wine with them, but I didn't tell Emma. She knew. From Winnebago, they took her to Omaha because she needed a caesarean operation. I rode along in the government car. When we got to Omaha, Emma was placed in a room. She had a very fine doctor, and I knew everything was going to be all right.

I had my return ticket back to Alliance, and Emma knew this. She also knew that I had run out of funds. She told me to return home because everything was going to be fine, but I stayed with her in Omaha a whole day and part of a night. I didn't want to leave Emma there and felt very bad about not staying, but I realized my children were home and my mother was watching them. I finally thought things over and decided it would be better to come home. I think the train back from Omaha left about eleven in the evening, and I got back to Alliance about seven in the morning.

This was 1965, and the black people were demonstrating on the streets in Omaha. I will always remember the night I walked from St. Joseph's Hospital in Omaha to the train depot. It must have been at least two miles away, and I got caught up in one of those demonstrations. In fact, the demonstration covered the whole two miles. After I got home, I heard over the news that they had demonstrated in Watts, California, as well as in Omaha.

The day after I got back, Hap Barton came over to the house and asked me if I wanted to work part-time for one of his bakers at the Delite Bakery. He knew that I was a drinker and, at this point, unreliable, but he liked me because I was a good baker and could do the job. I started to work for him, to about one in the morning, and at night, Connie would take care of the children. At that time she was probably thirteen years old. With every little bit of money I made, I'd buy groceries first, and the rest of it I'd drink up.

All the time that Emma was gone, another ten days, I drank wine heavily, and I knew then that I was addicted to the damn stuff. The next morning I'd be shaky and nervous; I couldn't think and would need more wine. I was really getting afraid. The day that Emma was supposed to come back from the hospital, they brought her to Pine Ridge. She called and told me to come after her. At that time I had a 1950 Chevrolet car, which I kept in pretty good repair. So I just quit drinking wine and went after Emma. Evidently when I got there, I was sober enough for her to think that I hadn't been drinking, when, in fact, I had been drinking all the ten days she was gone.

When I picked her and Hope up at the hospital, it made me feel so darn good that I just forgot about the wine, the lying, and all this stuff that I'd started to do. I brought them back home and will always remember carrying Hope into the house. I grabbed ahold of her and said, "Hope, this is your new home." She lifted her little face up and looked all over the house, like she understood what I said. It was remembering fine things like this that happened between me and my family that eventually caused me to sober up, but in the next three to four years, I went through hell.

The next morning I went out and got a steady job working on a farm. I worked there the rest of the summer making $1.25 per hour, which at that time was pretty good money. On weekends I would only drink beer, but it really didn't affect me, and I was able to continue working. Things were going well then, and I thought, maybe later on I can get back into the bakery business. I had a lot of good thoughts, and worked all of 1965 and part of 1966.

The lady who owned our house moved and sold it, so we had to move to a different place. When we started moving, I started drinking wine again. I always respected my mother, and I didn't want her to see me in this condition, but she caught me passed out inside our home. I had been hauling the furniture up to our new house and drinking wine when all of a sudden, I just got sleepy, lay down, and passed out. So when she woke me up, she went down and got me a double-dip ice cream cone and made me eat it so I'd have something else in my stomach. I felt awful that my mother saw me drunk and passed out like that, but nothing changed. Emma knew about my drinking all along, and she also knew that I was at the point that no matter what she'd say to me, I'd just keep drinking.

After we moved, Emma, Connie, and I got a job in a potato cellar. Connie's and Emma's job was to run a machine. They'd put a sack in it, so many potatoes would go into it, then they'd sew it up. It was a good job. The real small potatoes would come out of the end of the machine with the water; and I'd sack them, sew the sack, and pile them up. I was constantly wading knee-deep in water for the whole ten hours I worked. It was wintertime.

There were a lot of other Indian people at this potato cellar, and most of them drank on the sneak whenever the boss was gone. Everyone would manage to take a pint or a couple of pints to work with them. We did this for, I think, the whole winter of the latter part of 1966. I had a hell of a job; it would be ice cold outside, and when I'd come out, I'd be wet clear up to my knees. It's a wonder I didn't catch pneumonia. Evidently, I still had my health and was able to survive. Emma knew I was drinking on the sly, and she told me quite a few times that she didn't want me drinking wine any more. But I'd say yes, yes, and the next thing you know I'd be doing it again. Everybody was drinking there except Emma and Connie. I knew they weren't, but all the rest of us were, including a lot of the women; whenever we'd get a chance, we'd all drink.

One day the conveyor stopped, and the potato washers were all broken down. The boss came along and picked out eight of us guys to go ahead and load the potatoes into a boxcar. So we started doing that, and we loaded two boxcars of potatoes. Then we broke for lunch. The other guys were all saying, "Well, look, when we go in for dinner, one guy get a pint of wine, and the other get a quart." We were making our plans for that afternoon, as we had to load two more boxcars. It was a heck of a job. Some of us were outside, and some of us were inside. At that time I was able to handle a hundred-pound bag of potatoes as well as anybody else; just lift it up on your shoulder and throw it up in the truck or the boxcar.

We went in for dinner, but when we came back, the boss came up to me and said, "Mark, I'm going to have to lay you off because I got too many men out here now." I said, "Lay me off? Don't you want me to come back tomorrow?" He said, "No, laid off." I asked what happened. I had been working out there a long time, so I wondered why I was getting laid off. He never told me, but I found out later on that my brother-in-law, Orville, who was always snitching to the boss, had told the boss I was one of the guys out there drinking wine. He said I was the instigator of all this, which I wasn't. Other guys did more drinking than I did.

Anyhow, I lost my job, and Emma and Connie continued to work there. It was a blow to me. I didn't know that Indian people snitched on each other. I was getting my first lesson in Indian politics. So I stayed home and started being the housekeeper, but I didn't like it with Emma and Connie working and my becoming the babysitter and housekeeper. This started me drinking again, as much as three to four pints a day. Whenever I'd wake up in the morning, I'd be so damn sick that I had to have a drink. But in some of my more sober moments, I didn't want to be hooked on this wine. It was tough fighting it. When Emma and Connie worked, they'd buy groceries and pay some of the bills, but there was always money left over for alcohol. I didn't really know I was becoming addicted because when this was happening, there wasn't any dope in our town, no drug problem, and nobody knew about alcohol addiction.

For example, my brother and I recently were talking about delirium tremens. Butch recalled that we used to call them "snakes." People would say one of our friends was having the snakes because he drank too much. What they do is just tie them up and lay them in the corner somewhere until they got all right. We didn't know at that time that a man or a woman could very easily die when in delirium tremens. Alcoholism was something that we didn't know anything about. In my later years at Fort Meade, South Dakota, and Hot Springs Hospital, I started learning about addiction and all its problems. If they had had any alcohol programs at that time in Alliance, I might not have gone through all the torture that I put my own body through.

In 1967 when this was happening to me, I woke one morning up at six o'clock, and I was so damn sick and needed a drink so badly that I just got up and walked downtown. It was in the wintertime and probably twenty or thirty degrees below zero. We lived quite a way from town, at least fourteen to fifteen blocks. I didn't have any money.

After I got to town, I found several Indian people who were not my friends or people I had ever socialized with, and I kept more or less to myself. These guys I'm talking about were the derelicts in the park who did nothing but drink day in and day out. These are the guys who taught me the sharing of everything you have with another Indian person. When I met these guys, there were a couple of women with them, too. They were all waiting for the liquor store to open up.

When they saw me coming, they knew who I was and that I'd been kind of a snob most of my life, a hard worker, and a good family man. They didn't say anything, but one guy came up to me and said, "Mick, are you sick?" I told him, yeah, that I didn't have any money and was sicker than a dog and needed a drink. They had a couple of quarts. So we all drank together out in the alley. They knew that I was down and out, but they never held my good part against me. This was my first involvement with the Indian alcoholics' way of giving and sharing of alcohol, the same as they do with what they have when sober.

It may be that is one reason Indian people cannot stop drinking, because of their continuous involvement in helping and sharing. If one Indian alcoholic needs a drink and he can't help himself, well, his friends will give him drinks. It doesn't matter what social level one comes from. Indians treat the white winos this way, too. I suppose some of the women sold themselves to get the money. But, whenever they did, they would share with anyone who needed help. That's what happened to me. I said, well, heck, I know what to do from now on if I need a drink; all I got to do is go downtown. At that time, I didn't realize what I was getting into. That day I stayed uptown most of the morning and drank with the guys. When I left, they all pitched in and bought me a quart to take home with me so I wouldn't be so sick when I woke up.

During all this time that I was drinking and not working, I was just dependent upon my family. Emma had started to work as a maid at a hotel. She didn't like what I was doing and was totally against it. Even my children could feel it, and they were becoming ashamed of me. I was an alcoholic, and my body was beginning to show the effects of the wine and the drinking every day. I think my mind was even deteriorating at this time, too. My family never did reject me completely or ever give me hell. They just accepted it, or so it seemed. I'm very proud that I had this type of family because, if not, I'd have been dead now except for their care of me. I never chose to quarrel with my kids or pick on Emma; I was just a kind of a quiet, relaxed drunk. I can't remember any time that I ever abused my family, but if I had, I'd have ended my drinking career sooner than I did.

In the summer, I remember Emma went uptown with the kids, and they brought back chicken, watermelon, and potato salad. Emma fried the chicken. They probably thought I was sober, but I had some wine laid away and was drinking steadily. I was coming to the point where I could not eat. Terry, Daryl, Connie, Kandi, and Hope (she was a little girl at that time) were all sitting around eating out on the lawn. That meal and my family looked so damn good, and here I was sitting on the porch thinking to myself, how in the hell did I ever get into the shape where I can't even eat a meal with my family? I didn't know then that I had progressed so far into alcoholism that even the thought of food made me sick. I was sitting there so ashamed of myself and so ashamed over the loss of everything—my respect and self-pride. I don't know whether the children or Emma thought this way or not, but I did.

These are some of the things I later remembered vividly when I was in Fort Meade, South Dakota, for treatment, and I thought I had become a total maniac. My family supported me; even though I had become an alcoholic, I was their father. They would probably have done anything in their power to help me. God had his way of protecting me and helping me eventually to become what my wife once said was "the man that you were and will be."

One Sunday morning in the summertime I was very sick. I got up early and just left home without telling Emma where I was going. I suppose she knew that I needed a drink and went to get one. She never said anything about it, but I knew she was mad. That morning, I walked clear to the west end of town, two and a half miles away. Alliance didn't sell wine on Sundays. So I went over to a bootlegger's place and told him I'd like to have two pints of wine. They were selling for two dollars a pint. I had known this man for a long time, and he trusted me, so he gave me two pints, and I told him I'd pay him on the first of the month, which eventually I did.

As soon as I left his place, I went down the street drinking one of the pints up. I would consume it all and not care how sick I was, and if I had more wine, then I'd become more normal again. So I felt good. I went down to the park, saw some of my friends down there, and gave them what wine I had. Probably we were drinking the whole afternoon.

That night they were having stock car races east of Alliance, and I always liked to watch them. I liked to stand by the fence as the cars went around and around the race track. Toward evening one of the guys gave me another pint or even two pints 'cause I still had some wine left. I walked out there to the stock car races, which would be about another mile away from the park. I stood there watching and drinking. I was happy. I was at the point where I was forgetting all about my family. My only concern was for myself. I didn't like that either, but I stayed there and drank one pint up and threw the bottle away.

After the race was over, I started for home. I got as far as the park, went up to the street called Missouri, and started going west to Twelfth Street, where we lived at that time. I knew that I was sick, mentally and physically. The only thing I was happy about was that I had another drink. It was very dark. I very clearly heard something walking behind me, like a person who was following me. I was wondering if I needed protection because I was in pretty bad shape. Anyway, I thought, whoever this guy is, he's going to run over me, and I stopped. The street was very dimly lit, but I could still see. I turned around to look behind me, but there was nobody there. I wondered what was following me; I felt in my back pocket for this other pint of wine and took another drink. I don't know whether I was afraid, because I'm the kind of guy who doesn't believe in ghosts and spirits, but I was kind of wobbly and shaky. I put my bottle away and continued walking home.

I was probably at this point another ten blocks away from the house. I kept walking, and whatever this thing was behind me kept following. Once in a while, I'd look over my shoulder to see who it was or what it was, but there was nobody there. Whenever I'd start to walk, I could hear these footsteps and feel somebody behind me. It felt like whoever it was, was near me.

Finally I got up to Tenth Street, and that street was well lit by street lights. I stopped there for a couple of minutes. I think I was breathless and tired. I started again, and the footsteps started, too. At this point, I don't think I was getting scared, but thinking that maybe someone was taking care of me. So I just took my bottle out, took another drink, and started in walking again. I had four more blocks to go, and all the time I could feel some presence behind me. I got to our home, opened the gate, and started up the steps. When I got to the porch, the footsteps stopped, and the feeling of being followed left me. I drank up the rest of my bottle, threw it out on the lawn, and walked inside the house to where my family were all in watching TV. Everybody asked me where I was at, and Emma was very concerned about me. But I just lay down and went to sleep. The next day I started getting drunk all over again.

I think that what happened to me was some kind of delerium tremens. I think I probably was going to die on my way back that night, that's how bad my body and mental state were, how far I had deteriorated. Whatever followed me and protected me all the way to the porch of my home was what saved me that night. It kept my mind and body alert.

We lived on Twelfth Street, in a predominantly white neighborhood, but within one block there were five or six Indian families. In one of them was an elderly Indian gentleman named Jim Crow, who was about seventy-five or seventy-six years old and drank quite a bit. He always seemed to be able to completely sober up the next day. Whenever I walked past his house, he always called me in to have a glass of wine, or he'd give me a pint. I think he was concerned about me, too, because he was a very good friend and liked me. I think at this time Jim was observing how my life had changed from good to bad and that I'd been drinking too much and it was affecting my family. Although he was really concerned, he was afraid to talk to me about it. He just kind of minded his own business and helped me the way he thought was best by giving me another drink.

One day, a week or so after I had this bout with delirium tremens, I walked past Jim's house again. He called me into his home where he had a half-gallon of wine and poured me a glass. He started talking. "Mick, why don't you start sobering up now? You've been drunk for so long, maybe you ought to start thinking about it and becoming again the man you once were." He knew that I'd worked at the bakery and maintained a good family life. I respected Jim a lot. So I told him, "Jim, I know I'm very sick and I know what I'm doing to my family, but I just can't quit. I've got to have a drink every day." I told him the predicament that I was in. However, I felt better after talking to him, and that feeling of someone caring for me made me start thinking very seriously about what to do. But I didn't know who to go to or how to sober up, so I kept drinking and bumming and coming to a point where I could barely walk again. My arms didn't work, and my speech was so slurred I could hardly talk. My jaws seemed to tighten up on me. I was coming to the point where I just didn't care anymore.

One day I went down an alley and came to Jim Crow's house and looked in the back of his dumpster—actually, just fifty-gallon drums. I had started getting into the habit of looking into people's barrels to see if they had thrown away a bottle of wine or whiskey, and if there was anything left in it. If there was, I'd drink it. Jim saw me back there. He came back, and we sat down in the alley by his trash barrel and started talking. He was asking about my family and how I was doing. He looked at me and saw I was very sick and said, "Mick, you want a drink?" I said, "You bet, I'll take one." We walked inside his house, and he brought out a quart of wine. We sat down again by the barrel, right in the alley. I always remember Jim saying, "Mick, it's time you do something about your life." He told me what bad shape I was getting into, and said he hadn't even known me standing there by his barrel. He thought it was one of the bums off the train or someone rummaging for food.

Jim said, "Now, I don't know whether you're going to do it or not, but you should think about going to Fort Meade, South Dakota. They've got a treatment center there for alcoholics. All you've got to do is go down to the VA office and tell them that you want to go there for treatment." He just told me like it was.

I sat there with him and started thinking, my God, I'd gone this far, and what the hell am I going to do? At this time I was real fearful of going to a treatment center. This is because probably I was hooked on wine and didn't want to stop. So I told him, "Jim, I'm going to do something. I'm going to think about going to the treatment center." He started telling me what a good family I had, my wife, children, and all, and said, "Mick, I've known you; you've got it in you to do it. You know, in thinking about it, if you need a drink or you need any help, just come to my door, and I'll help you." I think this was my first involvement in alcohol counseling, which later in my life I did a lot of. I'm always thankful for Jim because he put the idea into my mind and with his coaxing caused me to do something about my drinking problem.

My mother and father were also very concerned about me, and they were giving me money to buy a pint or a quart of wine just to keep me from dying I suppose. One day I thought, I'm going to somehow figure out how much I'm drinking. Maybe I was coming to the breaking point, I don't know. That day, every time I'd walk to town, get a couple of pints, and walk home, I'd go into the bedroom after I'd finished, and I'd set the bottle up next to the wall. Emma never saw this. At this time, she was working at the hotel as a maid. I think I was coming on something that I still don't know how to explain, but it did me a lot of good. What I was trying to do is figure out how much I was drinking. I was at the point where even though I was sick and the wine had usually helped me, it didn't any more. It just made me sicker, but I still had to have it.

That night about one or two o'clock in the morning, I woke up, looked over against the wall, and counted the number of bottles I had drunk. There were twelve pint bottles lined up against the wall. The next morning when I woke up, I could not even get out of bed. My legs would not work. It just seemed like they were numb, and my arms were the same way. My jaws wouldn't move, and I had the most miserable feeling that any human being could ever get. Emma was lying next to me. I sat up somehow in bed and told her, "Go down to the sheriff's office or to the VA service officer and tell them that you want me committed to Fort Meade, South Dakota." I told her also, "Emma, before you go down, get me a pint of wine somewhere so that I can come out of this and at least walk, get up, and wash my face." Somehow or another, she bought me a pint, and she did go to the court house. At that time, I think she talked to the sheriff, who went to the judge, and they got me committed to Fort Meade.

C·H·A·P·T·E·R VI

A TREATMENT FAILURE
Fort Meade

When I went to Fort Meade, I was so scared and so fearful of what would happen. I thought I could never get along without wine, and that I would probably die. They called it a voluntary commitment, which made it look better. By the time the sheriff's deputy came to our house to pick me up, I was so sick that I couldn't even walk to his car, and I could hardly open my jaws to speak. Emma got me clean clothes to put on. Of course, we didn't have any money, so we didn't have anything I could take with me. I told the deputy sheriff, who was a young fellow I knew before this, that I would never be able to make it to Fort Meade and told him also what the problem was. So he said, "Mick, I'm going to get you there, but what would be the best way to do it?" I said, "Get me a couple of quarts of wine, and I promise you I will drink them slowly just to keep myself alive until we get to Fort Meade." He said, "It's against all our rules, but I'll do it."

He went downtown and came back with a couple of sacks. It was one of the worst days of my life, having to leave my family, yet I knew that I had to do it. Fort Meade is probably 230 or 235 miles from Alliance, directly north of Rapid City, South Dakota. We left, and to this day, I don't know how in the world I ever made it. I was so sick and so frightened. I couldn't even hold a quart of wine up to my mouth any more. When we arrived at Fort Meade, I was still able to think and know what was happening, even though my arms and legs and body didn't function too well. The deputy sheriff took me to the admitting office. I think all this time he was kind of halfway carrying me. I couldn't even give them the information about myself. Somehow he must have had my service record there so that I was admitted.

The aides came and took me to a ward, and a psychiatrist named Dr. Schneider was there. Dr. Schneider took one look at me and kind of shook his head and didn't say anything. But he started giving me a physical examination and feeling all over me, hitting my leg with a little hammer and my arms, too. At this point, I hadn't had a drink for probably two or three hours after the deputy had left there and returned to Alliance. What I needed most was another one. I told Dr. Schneider how I felt. "Well," he said, "first of all, we'll get you a bed."

He led me from one office to another in the admitting process. It was so torturous to me that even to this day, I don't remember how I made it. He started giving me some kind of tranquilizer, and I think I was taking something called Paraldehyde. I would take them as pills probably every four hours. I couldn't eat at this point, but he told me that chow was at a certain time. Every time he mentioned food, I would get so damn sick that I couldn't eat. That night I was put in a large ward with about thirty to forty men. I didn't know that these guys were all alcoholics and were suffering from the same sickness I was. I was really afraid and didn't want to bother them. I was completely helpless, with my body and mind not functioning well. With the pills and other medication, I soon fell asleep.

At Fort Meade, South Dakota, there is a program designed just like the U.S. Army. You wake up at six o'clock in the morning, go eat, and they give you some kind of job to do no matter how sick you are. So the next morning at six o'clock, I was awakened by the orderlies. I don't know if they ever realized how sick I was. I couldn't even stand up, my head was splitting, and my legs and arms wouldn't work, but I'd gone the whole night without alcohol, and the afternoon before that.

Somehow with some of the other men's help, I made it

down to the mess hall to try to eat, but I couldn't even stand in line. I thought I was going to have delirium tremens again. I was thinking to myself that I should never have done this because I felt I had jumped out of the frying pan into the fire. Somehow I made it through that day. I remember walking around crying because I couldn't do anything and was so helpless. Dr. Schneider continued giving me this Paraldehyde and some kind of a tranquilizer drug. They weren't working for me. Paraldehyde would make me feel high for about two to three hours. Then I'd get back to this sickness again.

I think I was there one day and a night, when, as I was lying in my bed thinking I was going to die, someone came to my bedside. It was my brother Butch. I didn't know he was in Fort Meade too. Butch had always been kind of a hero type in my life, but I hadn't seen him for a long time. He said, "Mick, what's wrong with you?" I couldn't even tell him. Some of the other guys around me said that I was terribly ill and suffering from withdrawal symptoms. Butch really felt bad. While he was sitting with me, tears came into his eyes to see me in this kind of shape. I was down to about a hundred pounds because of the lack of eating.

To this day, when I think back, I feel that if my brother Butch hadn't been there, I would have died because I just would have given up and not wanted to continue. Butch knew what was wrong with me because he was in an alcohol program himself and had to attend meetings practically all day long. He was in another building in another ward and had gotten permission from his doctor to help me.

I was in this terrible condition for about forty days. Tears would come out of my eyes, and I wouldn't know where I was or what I was doing. I was so nervous that I still couldn't eat. Butch would take me to the mess hall, we'd line up, and he'd get me food. I'd remember that I was there to get well, but I thought, I'm not getting well; I'm getting worse. I just could not function mentally or physically, and I'd barely make it through the day. I was excused from work and the normal things that the men did there. I was absolutely out of it. What I'd do, however, was walk. Butch would hold me, and we would walk and walk and walk. We'd do the same thing in the evenings after we'd go to chow. I'd started drinking a little milk, and Butch would cut up my food for me and help me eat. This happened for over a month. All this time I didn't even remember that my family was at home.

Fort Meade is a large installation. When Butch and a friend of his walked me after dark, we'd go to the stables, as there was an old cavalry unit there. They would talk to me and probably counsel me, too. Even after I started feeling halfway normal, I'd still lose my equilibrium and not walk straight. My nerves were so shot that I couldn't do anything. This was after maybe two months of being in Fort Meade, and with Butch's help and Dr. Schneider's, too. Everybody there, the orderlies who worked with me, were really concerned I couldn't come out of this withdrawal thing. Once in a while Emma would write to me, and Butch would read me her letters.

I remember at nights when we had to go to bed at nine, I thought I was going crazy. I'd get so nervous that I'd walk up and down the aisles and feel that I was going to die at any minute, and this really scared me. But I didn't know what kind of medication Dr. Schneider was giving me: Paraldehyde, I found out later on, just took the place of the wine. It continued to make me drunk. When its effects would wear off, I'd get this nervousness and DTs again. After I was up there for three months, I was in no better shape than when I got in the sheriff's car to come there.

Dr. Schneider had a policy on the ward that if you were there three months and were married and had a family, you had to go back on a leave to see your family. Dr. Schneider called me to his office and said, "Mark, I want you to go home for a few days." I was in such a state that I didn't know what in the hell the doctor was talking about. Somehow during this period of so-called recovery, I had forgotten that I had a family. I think some of the coordination had come back in my arms and legs, but I still wasn't normal yet. Dr. Schneider said, "Mark, you've got to go back to Alliance, that's my policy—after three months you have to make a visit home."

During that time, evidently, Emma had made arrangements to come and pick me up. I was home for a seven-day leave. I don't think Dr. Schneider, the staff, or my family knew that I was in worse condition after three months than I'd been before.

When I saw Emma and my kids, I started drinking again. My mother, father, and my wife were feeling so happy to see me. After the seven days were over with, I felt good when I drank. I felt myself coming back to reality and knew what I was doing. I had to go back on the bus to Fort Meade, and I told Emma, I'll make it. So I got on the bus and got as far as Chadron, Nebraska, where I ran into some winos, and I started drinking heavily again. Instead of their taking me up to Fort Meade, they brought me back to Alliance. Emma was very upset.

The next morning when I woke up, my mother and father came over and took me back up to Fort Meade and left me there. I talked to Dr. Schneider again, and he said, "Mark, I know you've been drinking. About the only thing you got out of going home is to see your family. That's what I wanted you to do. But you're going to stay here." I told him, "Dr. Schneider, I was very sick once, and I feel I'm in worse shape now than when I came in. I don't know what's happened to me, but it looks like I'm losing my mind." He said, "Mark, what we can do is, I can sign you in here for a lifetime commitment, or I can give you shock treatments, and pull you out of what's wrong with you." That scared the hell out of me. Shock treatments. I'd heard what they can do to you. I didn't want this. So I kind of settled down. I figured, well, I had better try as hard as I can to come out of this. I asked the doctor, "Why is my body so uncoordinated; my legs don't work, and I'm dizzy all the time. I feel like I'm going crazy. Why do I feel this way?" He never did answer me. I stayed at Fort Meade another three months, and I was getting kind of used to the routine, but I was never normal.

During the time that I was at Fort Meade, Butch must have been discharged and left for home because I never did see him around any more. I don't even remember when he left. Even though I was in terrible shape, no one, not even Dr. Schneider, seemed to know what kind of condition I was in. I found out later that Paraldehyde is half embalming fluid and half alcohol. So basically what they did was to keep me on a long drunk.

The Fort Meade staff there were really pushing Alcoholics Anonymous (AA) meetings. When I was there for the first time, Butch took me to one, but I was too sick and didn't know anything then. I never did attend the AA meetings because I felt they never did anything for me. The counselor who ran these meetings was constantly after me. He'd come to my dormitory and tell me to attend, and I'd tell him I didn't want to. This kept up for nearly all the time I was in Fort Meade. I remember to this day the serenity prayer and have said it quite a few times in my life, but as for the rest of it, I could never see where it helped a guy.

At the end of another three-month period I was sent home again, and the doctor told me at this time that Emma would not accept welfare. I was drawing 30 percent disability from the Army, which amounted to about eighty dollars a month. The doctor sent me home to try to persuade her, so that my family could live comfortably while I was recuperating. I knew that she was working at a hotel as a maid and that she had too much pride to go on welfare.

I talked to Emma and asked her to go on welfare, but she very definitely refused, as she was getting along well with the kids and just wanted me to recuperate so I could come home for good. I knew at this time that I probably wouldn't recover, as Fort Meade wasn't doing anything for me, and I was progressively getting worse. Of course, I didn't have the alcohol in my body at this point. But after I'd come back to Alliance, I started drinking very heavily again. At this point, I kind of saw in Emma's eyes and my children's eyes that they were beginning to give up on me. I'd been gone six months; it hadn't done me a bit of good, and they were still suffering at home.

One day my mother, Emma, and children were coming down the street in the car. My mother peeked out the window and said, "Micky, come here." I looked over and somehow, even though I was very drunk, I stopped and talked to them. Mom told me to get in the car and that she had a quart of wine for me. This really surprised me because Mom usually didn't do anything like that. So I got in the car, and we drove around while I was drinking this wine, probably half a pint in one drink. I blacked out, probably, and the next thing I remember I was back in Fort Meade, strapped to a gurney in the hospital part of the program.

Fort Meade is divided into about four or five different sections. Some are for mental patients, some for the hospital, and others for the lock-up. Usually all the alcoholics stay with the mental patients, but if you get sick, they send you to the hospital. If you become overactive and get mean, they'll send you to the psychiatry part of the place. If you get too mean, they'll send you to D ward, which is a lock-up ward.

I lay there alone for a long time, and finally an aide told me where I was. I asked him if I could have a cigarette, but he said I was in an off-limits smoking area. At times cigarettes were the only thing that would kind of calm my shakes. I thought, I'm probably going to die now because I've come to this point where I have to be strapped to a bed—I just cannot function in life anymore. Evidently this is what my mother and my wife thought, too. I lay there for one or two days. I don't remember taking a bath, or even combing my hair. Sometimes nurses and doctors would come to me, talk, and ask me questions, but I don't remember anything about those conversations.

The day that they finally unstrapped me and let me get up, I was so weak that I couldn't even sit. The nurse and doctor had to lift me up and sit me. Finally, I got on my feet and was taken to a bed that was assigned to me. I had gone without alcohol for this long, but when I started coming back to being a human being again, I asked the doctor for a cigarette. They took me to a little day room where the smokers could have a cigarette every hour. I didn't have any money to buy cigarettes, but at that time the VA would buy them for veterans. When the little cart went by every day, the doctor got me a pack. It was my allowance for the day.

I went to the room, had a smoke, and when I smoked a cigarette it seemed to calm my nerves. I thought, maybe I'm back to being myself again. I started thinking positively. When I started talking to the other guys and smoking with them, they told me that I had tried to break the straps quite a few times and would really fight the nurses and doctors and curse them out. I don't remember that. That's probably the reason they kept me tied up so long. Every place I went, a nurse or an aide had to go with me to hold me up because I was so darn weak and uncoordinated. I'd lost my equilibrium and couldn't walk right. Every hour when it was time to smoke, well, I'd go and smoke a cigarette and come back, and an aide or nurse would have to help me get back in bed.

They brought meals in trays, and I felt real comfortable that I didn't have to stand in the line with about two hundred fifty to three hundred men to get some food, as I had to when I first came to Fort Meade. I started picking at my food, eating a little, and drinking a little milk, but I never took a whole meal. I just didn't have any appetite.

One day the nurse came over to me and said, "Mr. Monroe, would you like to take a tour of our hospital wing here?" I told her, I'll do anything you say. I was beginning to become very calm. I was used to following orders anyway, so

I went with her. Afterward, I wondered if what I saw there was really true, or whether I was having DTs. She took me to a room where there were about ten beds and a crib. I saw a man lying in there. This little man couldn't have been over three feet tall. His facial features were those of an old man, and he just looked so bad to me. When I saw him, it scared me so badly that my mouth started tightening up and my jaws started locking up on me again. I became real nervous and afraid, but I had enough sense to ask the nurse what was going on. She told me this man had some kind of disease and that his body was shrinking. At one time he was a normal man. He never did say anything to me or the nurse, but she told me he had asked for euthanasia. In the state of South Dakota, if anyone asks to be put to death, the request has to go through state legislature and through the governor. They were in the process of doing it for this man because he wanted to die.

When I saw that guy lying there, the sickness that I felt when I went in the place kind of left me, and I felt very sorry for him. Somehow deep inside of me, it may have brought back some of my own fighting spirit or wanting to live and to get back to my family.

The next station we went to had a young man who couldn't have been over twenty-three or twenty-four years old. His legs were broken, and his arms, face, and head were in a case. The nurse told me that he had just returned from Vietnam. I didn't even know where Vietnam was, but I had heard about the war. She told me that this young man had come back from Vietnam to Sturgis or Rapid City where his home was and gotten into an automobile accident. He just completely crushed every bone in his body, including his head, but he was still alive. He was able to talk. He asked me how I was, and he could barely do this because tubes were sticking out all over him. He was completely immobile. One of his legs was tied up on a pulley holding it up. My God, I just absolutely couldn't believe what I was seeing.

This young man had also appealed to the state of South Dakota to be put to death, and his appeal was pending. There was absolutely nothing that could be done for him. I guess even his parents agreed that he should die normally. I understand now what was happening to this young man because later in my life my daughter Kandi was kept alive like this for two weeks.

Even though I was so mentally and physically ill, I knew right away what this nurse was trying to accomplish with me. I think she knew that if she showed me some people who were in far worse shape than I was, that maybe I would come out of this deep depression. Until then, I was fighting everything that they tried to do for me. This nurse, whose name I didn't know, was one of the very few people at Fort Meade who had any compassion for any of the patients. There were probably six or eight other guys who had become vegetables from drinking, and she let me talk to quite a few of them. There were some people also who were suffering from syphilis as well, and the only thing they could do was just lie there and look.

I think if the nurse would have told me, "Mark, look, we have some guys up here who are in far worse shape than you are. Quit your damn babying yourself and pitying yourself and continue with your life. You've got a wife and family at home. Come on now, try and get out of this thing you're in and be normal"—if she would have told me that at that time, I think it would have affected my life a lot different than what happened. Even though she didn't, I felt that she had tried to help me. If I'd had professional counseling, someone telling me what was going on and what I was doing wrong, I think I probably would have sobered up a hell of a lot sooner.

About a week after I started to become normal and realize where I was, Butch came to see me in the hospital. During this time he had gone back to treatment twice. Butch came to my bed and told me I was looking pretty good. He had been there when Emma and Mom and the kids brought me up, and he saw them tie me down on that gurney. He'd come every night to check on me, but they would never let him see me.

I didn't know whether Butch was back in Fort Meade because he was court-committed or whether it was voluntary. Fort Meade had restrictions on where the patients could go and when they could, but I believe Butch tried everything in his power to come and see me. I was in a very critical state when Mom, Emma, and the children had taken me back up. I must have been there three weeks or maybe a month before Butch could see me. He told me how worried he was about me and about the things that he saw. He didn't ever want to see me strapped in a bed again. I'm a very, very proud man. When Butch spoke to me, God, it made me feel bad, and I regret those things ever happening. I started to think. Why am I this way? Why do these things happen to me? Why did my family have to see me like this? After that time, Butch would come up whenever he got a chance. Sometimes it would be after five when he'd get done working. He'd sit and talk to me.

One day the doctor released me from the hospital, and I went to one of the buildings where alcoholics and mental patients all stayed together in wards. One day I asked one of Butch's friends, who lived in a different building two or three buildings away from mine, "Where's my brother?" He said Butch was discharged and went home. Dr. Schneider was still the doctor on my ward. He knew Butch was my brother, but he never informed me about Butch's leaving. At this time, I was still under lock and key, which meant that the only time I could go out was whenever the doctor would let me. Nobody could come and see me, or anything like that. God, this made me mad. So I always resented Dr. Schneider. I think I resented him more this time than I ever had before, as he was a psychiatrist who was also my doctor. I felt like I'd lost everything, and I again went into a real bad depression.

All this time, the man who was the counselor of the
AA meetings was coming to me and asking if I would attend
them. I told him, "No, I don't want to go." I think I had my
reasons. I was so damn nervous, and I knew I couldn't sit
still for the hour required.

At that time they built a new two- to three-million-
dollar hospital at Fort Meade. The people who were in the
older section were supposed to move from their living quarters to these new hospital-type living quarters. Everybody had
to push their own bed over to the new facility—a matter of
two blocks or so—and a lot of the people just couldn't do it.
It took us a couple of days because once we got our bed and
personal belongings over there, we had to go back and help
the other guys who weren't able to. This new building had so
many hallways and the wards were so complicated that I just
would get lost.

Well, we finally got ourselves moved, and I was assigned my new bed and developed a kind of routine of a pack
of cigarettes every day and go to eat at the mess hall. I
started beginning to accept things. Dr. Schneider told me that
if I didn't start following rules and regulations, he would sign
me in for the rest of my life, and he told me that he had the
power to do that. So I kind of figured I might as well stay
here and conform with these rules and regulations. Like the
rest of the patients there, I just kind of gave up and accepted
that kind of life.

Every ward had its own dayroom, and I'd sit in ours in
the evenings and feel very lonely. I'd come to the point where
I'd try remembering Emma, my children, and my mother and
father at home. I don't think I ever wrote a letter to them because I just couldn't write. Every once in a while, they'd take
me to this phone booth, and I'd call Emma, or she'd call me
up. I'd talk to her, and I'd forget right away what the conversation was about, but I knew somewhere back in my mind
that she had called me and that I had been talking with her.
Like the rest of the inmates at Fort Meade, I'd become a veg-

etable, following orders, drinking the medicine, and swallowing the pills.

One day I was sitting in the dayroom feeling very lonely, and this man was sitting there on the same couch with me. He was probably twenty years older than I was. He said, "Kid, what's wrong with you? Are you lonely?" I told him I was pretty lonesome and missed my family. He said, "Well, how long have you been here?" I told him I didn't really know. I told him what year I thought I'd come in, and he said, "Oh, hell, that ain't nothing! I been here twenty-seven years. I was in Honolulu, Hawaii, Pearl Harbor. My ship got sunk from underneath me, and I was caught trapped in it, and they brought me right back from Pearl Harbor and stuck me in Fort Meade, and I've been here ever since. There's quite a few of us up here. Fact is, the sheriff from your county has a brother-in-law that's been up here that long." We talked to some of the other guys, and I learned many of them had been here over half their lives in Fort Meade. I thought to myself, here I'm complaining about a bit longer than a year. It made me feel better.

So I started making quite a few friends. One night we were sitting around talking, and this one older guy said something about receiving shock treatments. He was telling us he received twenty-five to twenty-six of them. I talked to this guy, and he seemed like a really talkative person, but somehow, when you'd look at him, you could tell that there was nothing inside. He didn't have any mind; there was something missing, and it was frightening to be around him.

Later on I remember seeing on TV the film called *One Flew Over the Cuckoo's Nest*. Ken Lincoln in Alliance had lent me the book to read, and I had liked it. When I saw this film I thought, my God, this was exactly the way things were at Fort Meade. These were the exact guys I knew. Like the movie, we lined up for our medicine. I do remember standing in line for cigarettes and getting a free pack and drinking Paraldehyde and swallowing the pills.

As the days went by, however, I became very frustrated and angry because I wanted to go home, and I didn't think I was getting well. But I knew if I did leave, I'd get drunk again.

When Butch was still at Fort Meade, we'd walk around in the evenings, and we'd hear these noises from Bear Butte. It was near Sturgis, and we could see it. Before the coming of the white man, the Sioux had a lot of religious ceremonies over there, and they still do. Somehow or another, this was the only thing I felt good about. I felt that one time this was Indian country and Indian people had lived here. I think even Grandfather George Howard was at one time stationed near Fort Meade. I thought what I heard were yells from Indian warriors and distant drums beating. It never did really scare me but kind of gave me good goose bumps.

I think what really prompted me to escape from Fort Meade was this feeling of frustration and anger and wanting to go home. I knew the officials at Fort Meade were watching me very closely because I was not cooperating with them. I was just a bad patient, so I was on one of their watch lists. One whole week I'd go sit outside on the lawn in the evenings, and I would hear these Indian war calls and drum beats and other eerie type of noises. I was never afraid, the fact is, it made me feel more comfortable. I don't know whether it gave me courage or not, but one day I made up my mind. I think it was on a Sunday afternoon, as I was sitting out on the lawn looking at Bear Butte. I just said, well, hell, I'm going to go home. So I went inside the hospital and got a light jacket. This day, I looked in my pocket and found I had thirty-five to forty cents, and I was thinking if somehow I could get into Rapid City, maybe I could buy myself a little lunch. Without thinking twice, I just walked right out of Fort Meade.

Fort Meade is approximately three miles away from Sturgis, South Dakota. There was a creek running alongside the road, and I ran into the creek bed to avoid being seen and walked all the way to Sturgis. When I got there, I was real thirsty. I stopped in at a filling station and got myself a bottle of orange pop. I asked the guy which way it was to Rapid City. He was really looking at me closely because my hair was cut real short, and I had on clean looking clothes. I think I looked like a patient out of Fort Meade. So I drank my pop up and started walking out of town.

I walked for probably four or five miles down the road. Whenever a car would go by, I'd put my thumb up in the air and try to catch a ride, but no one picked me up. I walked along the road, and all of a sudden I could hear sirens somewhere. I looked back of me, and down the road was coming an ambulance with about two or three cars behind it. They came right at me and stopped, and about four or five aides jumped out and immediately put this straitjacket on me and put me in the ambulance. They took me back to Fort Meade.

I was wondering why they made such a big deal out of picking me up, but they took me down to our ward. Dr. Schneider was there, and he told me that I was going to D ward. I was going to be locked up for escaping, which he had warned me about, and he was going to sign me into Fort Meade for life.

I told him to go to hell and was very defensive. D ward is a lock-up for about fifty-five to sixty patients. A lot of the guys had their own rooms, but I slept in the dormitory part with probably thirty-five to forty guys. I think those confined quarters at that time did more to me than anything else they ever did at Fort Meade. I knew I was confined, and I felt like I was in prison. Most of the guys were mental patients. When I went in there, I was very scared, as some of these guys were absolutely insane. There was a great, big, black guy who had a hole in his forehead. Someone told me that they performed a frontal lobotomy on him. I didn't know what that was at that time, but I was always afraid of him. People who couldn't be handled normally were put into D ward, and some had been there twenty, twenty-five, thirty years. I figured I was better off dead than in there. It was my last hope, my last chance.

When I went into D ward, the patients right away came up to me and started calling me "Chief," which made me feel good. These were the nuts of Fort Meade, but they made me feel better than the people outside of the ward. The one thing that I really liked about it was that here we had small groups of men, and we ate right in the ward. Thirty men would go eat first. The aide would ask, are you a slow eater or fast eater, so I told him I eat normally when I do, and he put me last in the line. People who were slow eaters went in first, and therefore would have a longer time to eat. I liked this because there weren't too many of us in the building eating at one time, and everything was served to you. I started to eat, and I ate well. I felt comfortable there. Even though danger was present at all times because 99 percent of the people in there were mental patients, I felt good and at ease. I had this feeling, I'm confined here so I might as well enjoy it. That was my philosophy.

When I was in D ward, Emma sent me a brand-new pair of boots, as I'd worn my shoes completely out. All the mental patients came over, and they'd hold the boots like fondling a woman or something. Some of them even kissed them. It kind of seemed funny, but that's the way they were. They were just like a bunch of little children.

When Butch and I were in Fort Meade together, there was another Indian man about the same age I was. This young man had been in Korea and stepped on a land mine, which had blown off the back of his head. During his operation they had put in a metal plate, and evidently the mine had scarred up his back for he lost the back of his head. This young man named Pete Gurerue was from St. Francis, South Dakota. The only thing I remember really well about him was that he fought everybody in Fort Meade: the aides, the nurses, the doctors, and anyone who got in his way. He hated white people, and he was just a mean, mean guy. He wasn't much bigger than I was, but he probably outweighed me quite a bit. He liked me, but I always kept my distance from him.

One time during the night we heard a lot of guys talking loud, and the aides were hollering at somebody. Nobody got out of bed to find out what was happening. The next morning I woke up, and here they had Pete. They brought him in and locked him into one of these rooms that were padded, but you could hear him hollering and cussing. The next day I was talking to this aide whose name was Francis, and he was a real good guy. He was about the only aide that I liked. He told me that that night when they had brought Pete in from town, he tried to escape. It took about eight aides to bring him in and lock him up. I guess all this time he was still fighting. He was just a rough man, this Pete.

I was sitting in the dayroom, and I must have been the first one he saw. He came right over and sat next to me and told me what happened to him. He said he'd beaten the hell out of a lot of white men last night, and he was going to do it again. Then he started going around and challenging all of the patients in the dayroom. He was frightening. But nobody said anything, not even the black guy. The aides and nurses were just completely frightened by him. However, he sat down beside me, and I became his buddy right away. Whenever we'd go to smoke, he'd help me along. I didn't want to say anything or do anything to get him mad. After a while he calmed down quite a bit. He was Indian, and the only people he liked were Indian people, so I was in a good situation.

I'm pretty sure that I stayed in D ward at least four months and that these four months were very comfortable and rewarding for me. I still cannot figure out why I felt so comfortable there. Somewhere along the line the Paraldehyde was taken away from me. Anyway, I think it had been taking the place of wine, for I was just on a constant drunk all the time I was up in Fort Meade.

One day we were coming back from our dinner meal, and we went into the dayroom to smoke our cigarettes. As I said before, we smoked one cigarette an hour. All of a sudden a fight broke out between Pete and this black guy. Pete was beating him to a pulp, and I thought he was going to kill him. Everyone was afraid to stop Pete, figuring that maybe he would turn on them and beat them up, too. The aides were watching him, and pretty soon we heard a dull ringing, and down the hallway came ten, maybe fifteen, aides from other hospital areas, and they all grabbed hold of Pete at one time. They pulled him off this black guy and put him in a strait-jacket and into a padded room. It just seemed so scary that something like that would happen. All of us feared Pete so much we couldn't stop him from beating or killing a man. After Pete beat the black guy up and they had taken him into the hospital, I didn't see Pete again until a year later.

Now that I've been sober for so many years, I think the drugs I was given while I was in Fort Meade made parts of my life an absolute blank. To this day when I remember Fort Meade, I wake up in a cold sweat at night. The hatred I have for that place and for some of the things that I went through there is still with me. Like standing in the chow line and smelling the food that was being cooked, and the alcohol counselor who constantly berated me to attend AA meetings when I didn't even know what AA meetings were. I hated the confinement and all that Fort Meade stood for. When you go there, you're completely dehumanized.

But D ward today doesn't seem to be a part of Fort Meade, but a place where I was made to feel welcome and treated good by people who were there. Even though it was a lock-up ward where you could not get out after the doors clanged shut behind you, I liked the environment because I was treated with kindness. I learned how to eat again and to become self-sufficient to a degree.

For the past twenty years, I've been trying to analyze why I did not sober up at Fort Meade and why there was the span of time when I was released and got back to Alliance that I completely don't remember.

C·H·A·P·T·E·R VII

SOBER AGAIN
A New Life

T
he next thing I remember, I was back sitting on the front steps of our home in Alliance completely drunk, completely sick, and completely out of this world, you might say. I don't remember anything that happened, but I think it was August 1968 when a lady from the welfare office came up to me. Somehow or another, they finally talked Emma into receiving welfare checks because my family was in such a terrible financial situation. Emma had told this woman about the year I'd spent at Fort Meade and how I was not cured, not sober, and I was still drinking. I was barely alive. This lady came over at four or five o'clock in the late afternoon, and we sat down and talked. She was a very kind person. She asked me why I had been drinking and why Fort Meade hadn't done anything for me, as she knew how long I'd been up there. I think she was kind of surprised herself that I had spent so much time in a recovery center and still didn't remember anything and was still drinking heavily. She seemed worried and concerned about me.

She asked if I wanted to go to Hot Springs, South Dakota, to be put into the hospital there. I didn't associate Hot Springs with Fort Meade. Once before I had been in Hot Springs, probably in 1963 when I had a scalp irritation. I stayed there about a month, and I enjoyed it very much. I think I kind of argued with her at the time and said, "No, I don't want to go to Hot Springs," but again deep in my mind, I thought, well, I'd better go because I'm not doing any good here. Finally she said, "Mark, I want to take you. What can I do to help you realize that you have to go there?" So I told her I'd go, but I needed some wine to make the drive up there. I said, "I'm the type of person who has to drink, and whenever the drink wears off, I get so terribly ill that it probably would kill me." She told me to go inside, put on a clean shirt and pants, and tell my family where she was taking me.

I went inside the house. I don't remember who I talked to, whether it was Emma or the kids, but I talked to someone and said I was going to be hospitalized. I really wondered why I was doing this thing again, as I'd just spend a year at Fort Meade and wasted that much time of my life. The reality kind of hit me at that point. Once again, I wondered why I was still drunk, why I had to go through another recovery recuperation when it hadn't done any good before. I feared for myself and my family but realized I had to get out of the rut I was in.

So I got into the car with this lady, and she drove me to Hot Springs while I drank all the way up there. She was a very considerate woman. Whenever I told her I needed a drink, she would give me one. I was admitted about eight or nine o'clock that evening, and I was very intoxicated, but I do remember being put in a room. The doctor first gave me an examination, and I don't know what his diagnosis was or anything. I was too drunk at the time to remember what he said.

Immediately, the nurses and aides took me to a private room, and they closed the door. I went to bed and don't remember anything until early morning of the next day. I woke up and was so dreadfully sick. It's hard to explain how sick a wino can get. I was in such dreadful condition mentally and physically that I didn't even want to open my eyes. The only thing that I could smell was the wine coming out on my breath, and it was so hot, it was just hard to breathe. So I laid there: I wanted to pray but I couldn't, I was so scared at the time. I think I had a premonition in my mind that either I was going to die, or that this was going to be the last time I would go through a recovery period.

Pretty soon the nurse came in, and she wanted to give me some water and feed me, but I could not eat or drink. I could not tell her because whenever I would try to talk, my jaws wouldn't work. Evidently, this nurse had never seen an alcoholic in the type of condition I was in, and it kind of scared her. I was told later on that I weighed 108 pounds when I was taken to the hospital. My normal weight is somewhere between 165 and 170 pounds. I think this nurse was scared because I was just completely yellow; my eyes were yellow, and I didn't look like a human being. As I lay there in the bed, I began to become very, very fearful.

A doctor came in. I found out later his name was Dr. Murphy. I never could remember his first name. Dr. Murphy looked me over, and he was very astonished that I was in such bad shape. He said, "Mr. Monroe, I'm going to tell you something right now, and I want you to listen very carefully. I'm going to do all I can to save you, but your liver is so swollen that it looks like it might burst. You have yellow jaundice or hepatitis. If you do not quit drinking, you're going to die, and that's all there is to it."

After the doctor said that, it just added to my fears because this is what I was afraid of all morning. I knew that this thing had to conclude somehow. Everyone fears death, and this is what I was fearing. I knew that something had to happen to me because my life was wasted and that this was my last chance to live. Even though Dr. Murphy's remarks added to my fears, it did something for me, too. Somebody was concerned about me and wanted to do something to help me. Dr. Murphy told me exactly what was wrong with me and what was going to happen. I wished someone would have done this for me at Fort Meade one year before this. I somehow managed to ask Dr. Murphy where I was. By this time he was calling me Mark. "Mark, you're in Hot Springs, South Dakota. You're in the hospital and isolated in a room because we think you have hepatitis."

Not only was Dr. Murphy specific about what was

wrong with me; he went out of his way to spend a lot of time with me. I really enjoyed this even though I was deathly ill. I think that Dr. Murphy's being near and being interested in me and concerned kind of took some of the illness away. I remember asking him, "Dr. Murphy, are you going to send me back to Fort Meade, South Dakota?" He said, "Mark, I looked at your records, and it seems to me that you spent a lot of time up there. Why didn't you ever sober up? Whatever happened to you?" I told him the best I could, starting back from the beginning when I entered Fort Meade until the time I was released. He asked if they hospitalized me and ever took a physical or what else they did. The only time I remembered was when I was in the hospital there being strapped to the bed. Every time they would release me, I would get drunk again. Dr. Murphy was really amazed at how I could spend so much time in a recovery center and not be cured. This was what he was very concerned about.

I asked him again if I had to go back to Fort Meade, and he said, "Mark, I'm not going to send you back there. I'm going to keep you here in this hospital, and as I told you, I'm going to do my best to help you recover." When he said that I didn't have to go back to Fort Meade, somehow I became so relieved and trusting of Dr. Murphy that I could feel deep inside myself I was going to get better this time, and I felt good about it.

With my physical condition, I couldn't eat all that day. Maybe I drank a little water, or maybe a little juice, but the nurses caught up on it right away. Whenever the aide would bring me dinner or something, I'd leave it on the tray. The aide must have told the nurses, and the nurses told the doctor, for there was a lot of communication between them and a lot of caring. Dr. Murphy started talking to me. "Mark, why aren't you eating?" I told him I just couldn't do it. Somehow I made him realize that I could barely open my jaws enough to say no or yes, and even that hurt me.

Dr. Murphy took time out and called the nurse in and

gave me another physical examination. He started asking me
more questions, and I answered him the best I could. He already told me about my enlarged liver. When I looked down
at my chest, I could see my liver swell up between my two
breast plates. Dr. Murphy said, "Mark, you have to eat." So
he sat down beside me. I think that day we were served meat
and vegetables, but I was so darn sick I couldn't even look at
them. Dr. Murphy sat by my tray, cut the meat into very
small pieces, and did the same with everything else. He
started spoon-feeding me. He'd take a little piece of meat and
put it in my mouth. If I couldn't work my jaws, he would
take them and work them up and down to help me. I
couldn't swallow. Dr. Murphy never said what caused that,
but if I couldn't swallow the food on my own, he'd rub my
throat and kind of hit me until I did.

That first meal Dr. Murphy fed me must have taken an
hour. When he left, I thought, my God, how can one man do
this much for me? Even though I was very sick after I ate,
this feeling of someone being concerned and caring made me
try to eat and get well to go back to my family. They gave
this type of inspiration and hope at Hot Springs.

At supper time Dr. Murphy came in again and did the
same thing. He fed me, and he would take the glass of water
or the glass of milk and hold it up to my lips until I would
swallow it. I wasn't doing this to try to fool anybody as I absolutely couldn't do anything for myself. Dr. Murphy probably realized this, and for at least two weeks he helped me eat.
I started feeling guilty because I knew Dr. Murphy was so
busy. He had a lot of other patients to see. I got to thinking,
when does this man take time off, what does he do? I became
concerned about him.

Finally, after two weeks I got to the point where I
could at least sit up in bed and move my arms and legs. I lost
the hot breath that came out of me, and my mind began to
come back. I started realizing where I was, what was happening to me, and that I had a doctor who was so concerned

about me. From that moment on, I began to recover. Dr. Murphy was the most wonderful man that I ever met in my whole life, and I owe my recovery to him.

After I began feeding myself, Dr. Murphy said, "Mark, eat slowly, drink slowly," and he started to teach me all this. He also told the nurse that any time I wanted a chocolate malt or ice cream, she was to give it to me. After four weeks of drinking malts and eating my meals and listening to Dr. Murphy, I think he began to feel good, and I started to feel happy myself. Somewhere deep inside of me, something wanted to live again.

From that point on, I became human. My health started to come back, and I began remembering all the good things about my life. After about thirty days the nurse told me, "Mr. Monroe, your wife is here and wants to see you." She said that I'd have to go to the door and talk with Emma outside because I was still in isolation with hepatitis. When my wife saw me, she was so happy and relieved. I think she realized how much I had improved this time here in isolation and what Dr. Murphy and the nurses had done for me. I must have shown that improvement. When I saw how happy Emma was, I felt so good. In my mind, I knew that Emma had been right when she said to me one time, "You're going to be the man that you once were, and you're going to do it." It felt like coming back from the dead and being revived at that door.

I remembered the suffering that I had gone through to come to that point and the pain I had caused her and my family. I remembered the time strapped in a bed at Fort Meade and being near death. Somehow I felt inside of me that it's time, it's time after all this suffering that I rebuild my life, become a sober person, go home, and take care of my family.

Emma and I didn't get to talk very long, but I saw in her eyes her confidence in me. She had her mask on, and I had mine. I looked out of the window, and there were the kids all standing down in the street. I waved to them, and I think they saw their new dad again. Even now, whenever I feel lonely now that Emma's gone, and I think all of a sudden that I ought to get drunk, I'll have these flashbacks about how tough it was to get sober, and it will immediately stop me in my tracks.

Emma stayed there as long as she could before leaving Hot Springs to go back to Alliance. She started writing to me, and I think that when I came to my senses the nurse brought me all the letters from her. I had not even been able to read or open them for four weeks. It kind of gives you an idea of how far gone I was, how bad off in mind and body that I couldn't even hold a pencil up to write a letter to my wife. I did a lot of thinking there in isolation.

Dr. Murphy saw my medical sheet from Fort Meade, and he'd ask me if I could remember anything during the time between leaving Fort Meade and being drunk again, but I honestly didn't. He saw all the medication I was given and kind of shook his head in disbelief. After the first day I was in Hot Springs, I was taking a capsule. It was twenty-five milligrams of Librium. From the second day on, I remember that I was much calmer and less afraid. I asked Dr. Murphy how long this drug had been in existence, and he told me quite a while, and I couldn't understand why they didn't give it to me in Fort Meade. It helped me be calm enough to talk and feel alive.

Dr. Murphy said, "I don't know why they didn't put you on Librium, Mark, because Librium is an anxiety drug, and anxiety is what is happening to you. Anyway, it's working; we'll keep you on it. Even after your discharge here, I'll prescribe the drug for you. Stay on it until the time you think you don't need it anymore, which could be in a year, maybe two years." I think it was the kindness, concern, and friendship that Dr. Murphy and this nurse had shown me, plus the Librium, that helped me so much.

After about forty days in isolation, I was moved out to

the main ward with about twenty-five or thirty other guys; they were looking at me and were afraid to come near me because they all knew that I had been in isolation for hepatitis. They were a little distrustful of me. They probably all figured I was going to die, but I had made it. It kind of upset me at first and took away some of my pride and my ability to want to live again. However, I just made my bed, ate my meals, and did the best I could because I wanted so badly to get my health and sobriety back.

During this time Emma would drive up and see me with the children. At this point, I was able to go outside even though I was still weak. At least I could walk, go to the PX with my family, and tell right away in their faces how proud they were of me. I felt so good just looking at them. I knew how much I'd lost and that I was regaining it. I stayed at Hot Springs until my discharge on November 28, 1968. When I left, I was able to function well and was whole again in body, mind, and spirit.

I returned to Alliance and once again became a productive, sober human being. Now that I've been sober for these many, many years, I can't ever stop wondering why a man would have to go through this type of torment, torture, and living in a snake pit before sobering up, losing years of his life. When I think back on all the things that could have been done for me if there had been any interest, or any concern, maybe I could have sobered up much faster than I did. Now that I've worked in alcohol programs, I've helped design a couple of them for Indian people. I really don't blame Fort Meade for all the things that happened there, because in the years from 1960 up until the time I sobered up in 1968, there were no alcohol programs per se. I feel through personal experience that the alcohol programs and Alcoholics Anonymous meetings were not designed for American Indians. There is such a complete difference between the two types of alcoholics. Part of the difference is cultural. When I was in Fort Meade, I didn't know that alcoholism was a disease, and

I don't think they were equipped to handle a person with the problems I had.

Many of our Indian alcoholics in Alliance are still going through the snake-pit type of recovery that I did and never sobering up. I know men and women who have been drinking for years and who started in the 1950s and 1960s who have not recovered yet. When I was a patient at Fort Meade, I don't remember whether racism was a part of my life or not. The only thing I do know is that I wasn't ever given any consideration or sympathy. They thought they were doing their job, but from my point of view it wasn't until I entered Hot Springs Hospital as a patient that I met a doctor who showed sympathy, concern, and understanding for an Indian person.

One of the programs that I designed myself in 1970– 72 was strictly for American Indian alcoholics. My first concern in the recovery for my people was to humanize each man and woman. When I say humanize, I mean provide shelter, clothes, and food for each person so that he or she can recover physically and mentally first. All of the people I know here have lived through the same conditions, being treated as second-class citizens. Even though we did go to school, we never received our diplomas. This type of atmosphere affected our Indian people. It has been a degrading and dehumanizing experience for us.

The only way to work with the type of people I'm talking about is to show them a lot of concern for their disease. These are the steps that I would recommend. After the patient develops the physical and mental parts of his body, then you can bring forth whatever type of AA literature you think will work. This is one way. The other way that I would like to see is to let American Indians develop their own program in the simplest terms possible that could work. Organizers and the people who develop alcohol programs today forget that the large percentage of our Native Americans have not gone to school. They are not educated and so are not able to

read or to understand the literature that's given to them at
AA meetings or in treatment centers. So the literature can't
do them any good. I say, let's develop material that will help
the American Indian cope with alcoholism, and put it in simplest terms. Let's develop some films showing the Indian alcoholic lying in the park guzzling wine, throwing up, having
DTs, lying in an abandoned car sleeping at night, or crawling up and down the alleys looking in garbage cans for food.
If this is done on film and shown to Indian alcoholics, they
will understand.

During my sobriety when I started AA meetings, we
used to get films from the University of Nebraska. One of
these pictures showed a rich white lawyer who was an alcoholic drinking Scotch whiskey. It also showed his fine home,
his children dressed up real nice, and him getting into a large
Cadillac. Our Indian people who were attending the AA
meeting said, "Well, good for that son of a bitch. He's an alcoholic. Let him suffer." These Indian people were suffering
from the same disease, but they could not identify with that
lawyer and his high standard of living. It is foreign to Indian
people. The life styles of Indians and rich whites are so far
apart. This is one of the things that I see wrong with our
present-day alcohol programs. They do not include the American Indian—his poverty, his lack of education, the racism
that exists in our areas, which adds to the problem.

In the 1970s, we had meetings here at our Indian center in Alliance, and we talked with many alcoholics from
Gordon, Rushville, Hay Springs, Chadron, and Scottsbluff,
the larger Indian communities in western Nebraska. I saw
some of the things that were happening to the American Indians who were not able to sober up. I learned that one of
the main reasons Indians became alcoholics has to do with
education. One of the biggest problems was that up to 1954
the Native American was not allowed alcohol. We weren't allowed to drink it, we weren't allowed to possess it; it was a
federal law that we not have alcohol. Through my own per-

sonal experiences, I think this was a primary reason for me to be that way, to be an alcoholic. I never did learn how to drink.

The reason I say that is what I remember about my dad's life. My father liked to drink. My father was a hard-working, hard-drinking, hard-living man. He worked all week, and on Saturday nights he liked to have a drink. But now that I remember and think about my father, I always wonder how he managed to work and drink like he did. I had an example, too, and I lived partially that way, but not as hard as my father did. When dad wanted a drink, of course, he would have to find a white man or a Mexican or a black man to buy the liquor for him. If whatever particular drink he wanted cost three to four dollars, he would have to pay his bootlegger—this black, Mexican, or white man—the three and a half or four dollars and also three and a half to four dollars for the whiskey.

After all this trouble of getting the drink, when he would bring it home, he wouldn't be able to sit there and drink this alcohol normally like other people probably do, sip it and enjoy it, because he was afraid of being arrested or of someone turning him in for having alcohol, so he would go to the back of our yard and drink his own drink on the sneak. I know sometimes he'd take a pint of whiskey and in four gulps he would drink it up. He had to drink this way because of the federal law. I know now that the large consumption of alcohol at one time causes addiction to alcohol. Addiction is alcoholism. I think because my father never ever got the privilege of learning how to drink alcohol the normal way, he became an alcoholic.

The very same thing happened to me. I saw my father drink this way, and I drank this way for fear of getting caught by the authorities. I loved alcohol, but I knew the federal law said I could not drink it, so when I had it, I had to consume it immediately. To this day I think that that was the number-one reason why I became an alcoholic. Even though the alcohol act denying Indian people the use of alcohol was repealed in 1954, we all drank this way out of habit. Very few of our young people who are beginning to go to bars have learned how to drink socially. So they consume large quantities of alcohol. I don't know which is more important—to have a program that would teach Indian people to drink socially, or to to have a program that would help them quit drinking. As for me, I've learned not to drink, and I plan to continue my life that way.

In the early 1980s I helped write a proposal to start an Indian halfway house for the recovery of the Indian alcoholic. One of the things the Indian alcoholics, Ken, and I would ask our people when they entered our Center program is whether they want to learn how to drink or to stop drinking. When we talked to Indian alcoholics about this, three-fourths of the guys were honest and said, "Well, you know I like to drink, all I want to do is learn how," but three or four of them said, "Look, I want to quit. I'm tired of suffering."

Out of my own experience at Fort Meade I learned that when you have to do something, when you are given no choice, you don't want to do it. That is why I proposed to the group here that we put in the provision that for the people who wanted to quit drinking, we would dispense wine at eight o'clock, twelve o'clock, four o'clock, and maybe also at nine or ten o'clock at night. We hoped that if these alcoholics knew they had to drink wine at certain times, they would eventually get tired of it and quit. When this was brought up in discussion, a lot of the men answered that it would probably take all the fun out of drinking and maybe it would work. I hoped that it would for those who wanted to learn how to drink socially.

I'm sure if we'd had the chance to try out this type of program, a lot of things would probably have worked. No one ever tried them because nobody has ever been concerned about Indian alcoholics. I read in one of our newspapers that the incidence of alcoholism is as high as 70 to 80 percent in our Indian population. In the states of Nebraska and South Dakota they have programs that work for white people only. At one time we set down all of our ideas in a proposal, and I submitted it to various church, state, and government agencies, but any mention of the use of wine in a program immediately shuts off their concern and interest. Over and over again, this reaction just proved to me the complete lack of awareness of our cultural differences.

The American Indian has been stereotyped for so long as drunk and lazy that this is the way most white people see Indians. I don't want to see it continuing to happen because I know what it does to a human being to be labeled like that, to be degraded and compared with an animal. From the age of eleven clear up to the age of sixteen I would see those signs that would say, "No Indians or dogs allowed," and I'd find myself really thinking, "My God, I must be an animal; people are saying I'm a dog. I can't go in there because a dog can't go in there." To this day the existence of this kind of sign still bothers me. The degradation of racism was also one of the reasons why I drank. I couldn't find out really what I was.

Was I an animal? Was I a human being, or what? I went through all my young life, all my Army and adult life, wondering about it, and I still do. Why do people want to degrade and dehumanize us? I believe it was a psychological approach that the white people used to assert their superiority. It worked on me. I am sixty-three years old, and sometimes I still find myself wondering what the hell I am, a dog, a human being, or whatever. It's even harder when you look down at your skin and your skin is dark brown, and you're not white like the rest of the people.

I think another psychological reason for Indian alcoholism is the lack of jobs, the lack of coming home to a community. I know that when our Indian people do sober up, they find no support from their own people. When 85 to 90 percent of the Indian community is drinking, well, they think, that's the proper thing to do. Whenever one of these Indians sobers up, then they are no longer welcomed back into the drinking community. That makes it hard for the Indian people who want to sober up. Then when you come back into a town like Alliance, Nebraska, which didn't want you in the first place, and find there are no jobs offered you, no homes offered to you, no support offered to you, why sober up?

Indian people all over northwest Nebraska, not just in Alliance, but in towns like Chadron, Rushville, Gordon, Crawford, and Scottsbluff, face these conditions where they aren't wanted. The town will not offer an Indian a job nor rent an Indian a home. The conditions are made so bad that Indians become subhuman. Whenever people become dehumanized, that's when they drink and do bad things. If these towns were more accepting and people would treat Indians like human beings, then Indian people would act just like everybody else, and there wouldn't be a problem.

Whenever I see Indians here in Alliance who have just come off the reservation, I feel very sorry for them. I know that this man or woman has to be very strong. They want to work, and go look for a job, but usually there are no jobs available. If there is a job, then it'll be a menial one like shaking hides or working on the lawn or in the fields. If you go to rent a home, they'll give you the worst home they've got and charge you the highest rent.

These are the conditions that affect Indian people not only in western Nebraska but in the entire United States. I know it's happening in Colorado. And not only to Indian people; it's happening to blacks, Mexican people, and Asian people as well.

I don't know when the United States will ever become a democratic country. It doesn't look like it will ever happen because there are too many people who hate color. It's very hard for white people to understand that we all have to live together.

Let me give an example of what this racism does. In

the early 1970s, when I conducted a lot of alcoholism programs, I drove to Gordon, Nebraska, many times. This is where Raymond Yellow Thunder was killed. I didn't know him or get a chance to meet him, but he was, from what I've heard and what I've read in the paper, an example of how white people mistreat Indians. Mr. Yellow Thunder was one of the poor and unfortunate people who lived in these border towns with the whole white community disliking him and degrading him. He was stripped naked and thrown into the American Legion Club in Gordon in front of all of the white people who were standing there. They degraded this man so much that even if they hadn't killed him right then, he probably would have killed himself for how much he was degraded. He was killed because of some racist people who thought it was a game they were playing.

The people who killed him were the people who have this Ku Klux Klan attitude: If you're not white, then you don't belong and we will degrade you, we will dehumanize you, before we kill you. To this day I still don't understand it.

In Alliance, where I live, an Indian lady was found in our dump, dead, but no one ever investigated. No one knows who did it or why. It is just one of the things that happens. Indians are beaten; they are thrown out of places; they're degraded. Now people ask why Indians are in the situation that they're in. It is because of what happens in our local communities. The lack of understanding of other human beings. The lack of respect of other human beings causes this, and it'll continue to happen because we are such a minority in these areas.

I've worked very hard for years now to try to find ways to sober up American Indians and to keep them sober. However, so far, I've met nothing but a negative attitude from the people who are most in a position to help us. Now I'm very fearful that what happened to me will just continue to happen to a lot of our Indian people. There are quite a few who have sobered up in Alliance. Every one of them has asked me, "How did you do it?" And I'd tell them about the disgraceful things that happened in my life, and I'd also tell them how conditions did get better. I feel that one day someone is going to read these proposals and find that there is a complete difference between Indian alcoholics and non-Indian ones. If finances were available, the American Indians in this locale could develop a program, and we could stop a lot of suffering and misunderstanding. We could produce some sober, productive Indian people.

Some people ask if we ever use traditional Indian methods to treat alcoholics. I've worked with the Indian alcoholics for the past twenty years, and I've never used any Indian methods—sweats, the vision quest, Sun Dance, fast, Indian prayers. The reason I didn't use them is I didn't know how, and the people I would be working with don't know anything about it either. The American Indians living off-reservation, even some living on-reservation, are people who are living in two different cultures. We're brown people with a very beautiful culture that isn't wholly practiced now. We found that the only way to survive is to live in a white culture. So we don't know enough about our own. Many of our people, I'd say anywhere from 80 to 90 percent of our people, don't know how to speak Indian. They don't remember the Rabbit Dances, the Omaha Dances; they don't know what vision quests are. So even if I knew how to do them, I would never be able to use these because no one else understands them. It's very unfortunate, but Indian people are people who belong to one culture but have to live in another.

In my working with Indian alcoholics, I found that the only thing that works with them, no matter how jealous they are of you or how much they hate you, is to set an example. If you don't act above anybody else, then you're accepted as an Indian, but once you have become better, such as when I sobered up and became a human being, you are really not well-liked. But the thing that I've done is to sober up and set an example, and now after twenty years, I think our Indian people are saying, "Well look, Mark Monroe can sober up and he can do good, and I want to be that way." Even though it takes years and years to do it, I think it's working, because I have been able to help and talk to a lot of people even though they dislike me. It is a matter of the example that I have set.

Nothing in standard alcohol programs works for the Indian person. The literature that Alcoholics Anonymous sends out, we don't understand. The drinking programs that they have are no use to us because we just use them, come out, and get drunk again. I think that an Indian person, to help other people, just has to set that hard example that says even though I am Indian, I am sober, I am a human being, and I'm trying. I think this is what other Indian people are seeing in me, and even though it has taken many, many years, it is working.

Over the years I've helped at least twelve Indian people to sober up. I think my experience with alcoholism is a good example. I'm thankful I had a doctor who understood my problem. As I said, I don't think Dr. Murphy was the type of man who saw color. He just knew how to handle a human being. When I came back to Alliance, I knew the color factor was here so I had to use his type of tactics because there aren't too many people around like Dr. Murphy. But I do know this: concern and understanding does work. As a result of the type of support and backing that Emma, my children, and people like Dr. Murphy and his nurse gave me, I've been able to start a lot of self-help programs that provide direct services for low-income people regardless of race or creed.

Even though I've been sober for around twenty-three years now, I don't feel like I'm done yet. There is still so much to do. What God put me through, he had a reason for. In the past eight years I've had every reason in the world to get drunk again, losing my oldest son, Terry, my wife, Emma, our middle daughter, Kandi, and having several strokes myself. But I don't ever want to drink again. What happened in the past was God's way of teaching me. It was a terrible experience I put myself and my family through. But I have come to a new lease on life, and I feel happy and proud of it. I know it can be done.

In America we have all kinds of people, Indians, whites, blacks, Asians, and all have a different type of culture. White-dominant society has all its programs built for their particular culture, but these programs do not work for all. Hopefully somewhere down the line, somebody's going to understand and say, "Look, you know Indian people have a way to develop their own program that will work for them. Let's give them a chance and help them to become productive, sober citizens again."

Butch (eight years old) and Mark (four years old), Martin, South Dakota, 1935

Brother Bill's wedding: Aunt Lena, Pricella, and Butch (*back row*); Bill Monroe, Sr., holding Bobby, Minnie, Mark, and Emma (*second row*); Mary Ann, Veronica, Bill Monroe, Jr., Fontaine, and Father Manning, Alliance, 1952

When Mark was in treatment: Connie, Emma, Kandi, Daryl, and Mark, Fort Meade, 1967

Group representing the
American Indian
Council: *Clockwise
from front center:*
Donna Flood, Hope
Monroe, Irene Flood,
Governor Tiemann,
Connie Stairs, Mark,
and Loretta Lopez (*far
right*), 1969

Boy Scout Troop 274,
Alliance, 1970

Boy Scout Troup 274,
Indian dancers,
Alliance, 1970

Terry Monroe,
champion dancer, with
Pat Exon, the
Governor's wife, 1970

Minnie Howard Monroe, Mark's
mother, 1972

Emma Monroe, 1976

Mark and his father, Bill Monroe, 1976/Courtesy of Kenneth Lincoln

American Indian Center, Nutrition Program: Mark (*standing*), Bill Monroe, Sr. (*seated, far left*), c. 1976/Courtesy of Worley Studio, Alliance, Nebraska

Emma holding Shannon and Mark holding Terry, 1979

American Indian Center, Thanksgiving, 1979

Mark and Butch, 1986

C·H·A·P·T·E·R VIII

AN INDIAN CANDIDATE
FOR PUBLIC OFFICE

When I returned to Alliance in November of 1968, after being in Hot Springs, I was sober, and things seemed so different to me. It was the first time I'd been sober with my family for a long, long time. Getting adjusted to being back home was hard at first, but I was so happy and so proud of myself and my family that it seems as though I wanted to begin my life all over again. After thinking about what I'd gone through and how I'd recovered, it gave me kind of a momentum, you might say, to really do something.

Emma told me that during the spring or summer of 1968, they put her on welfare because I was drawing very little in compensation pay for my Army disability. My wife was a very proud person, and she did not want to become a welfare recipient; I think it kind of took some of her pride away, and mine, too. But I was so happy to be sober again that I just accepted it, and we continued to stay on welfare as long as I still was not in good enough physical shape to get a job. Deep inside me, I was really wishing that they would cut the checks off. I don't think it amounted to much money, but it was just the idea of it.

At that time Community Action was a very important part of Alliance. It was the federal program that worked with low-income people. One day, I noticed an advertisement in the paper saying that the Community Action program needed a center director, so I went uptown and applied for the job. This must have been in December, maybe a week and a half or two weeks after I got home. Before this, I had looked around to see if I could find some type of job that was suitable for me. I couldn't do too much work because I wasn't quite strong enough yet. They told me at the center that they would be interviewing people who applied sometime in January. So I signed up.

In the meantime, whenever I'd go to town, I felt so ashamed that I'd done something really terrible in my life by becoming an alcoholic and this gutter-type person. A lot of my true friends, both white and Indian people included, were very happy to see me and see that I was sober. However, there were many Indian people who wouldn't even talk to me. The Indian people saw me sober, and they would immediately tell me some of the things I had done when I was drunk. They were just mad that I was sobered up and would not accept me back as a friend. So it was hard for me to go around town and hard for me to talk to them, as ashamed as I was of what I had done. But I was so proud of my sobriety that I just said to myself, I'm not going to drink any more, and I don't care what happens to me. I'm going to stay sober, stable, and maintain my family life.

One day, as I was walking back from the Community Action Center, which was probably a mile or mile and a half away from where we lived, I saw this poster stating there was going to be a city election for police magistrate. I knew the present one. Her name was Mrs. Nell Johnstone, and she had been in office for twenty-five years. She was a college graduate and a very important person in Alliance. Her father was one of the old founders of Alliance, and Mrs. Johnstone had the reputation of being a fair judge. I had gone before her at least three or four times during my drinking days. She always asked me if I was guilty or not guilty, and I'd plead guilty, so she'd give me a fifteen-dollar fine. I knew that she was fair, but she did not want to do anything for alcoholic people.

I remember back one morning when I woke up in the city jail on a Sunday and there were twenty-seven people in jail in a very small twenty-by-twenty-foot room. They were all Indian people. The city of Alliance had a trash system where the truck with three to four Indian prisoners behind it would pick up the garbage barrels and throw them into the trash truck, and two more guys would throw them back out to be refilled. Even though Mrs. Johnstone knew these things and that she had a large number of Indian alcoholics in jail, she never made any attempt to try to rehabilitate them. It was just a day-to-day job she had of fining Indian people, giving them a place to work, and getting the city of Alliance labor free of charge. When I saw this election poster, right away, I felt that maybe if I were to be elected, I would be in a better position to help a lot of alcoholics, Indian and white alike. All of them needed some type of recovery program built for them.

I really was thinking seriously about this, so I went home that afternoon and thought about it that night and finally decided to run for the office of police magistrate. However, I was kind of scared, too, because this would be the first time in northwest Nebraska, and probably the entire state, that an Indian had run for an elected office. I knew also that it would be very hard to be accepted in Alliance as a political candidate. But I talked it over with Emma that night and told her that the next day I would go to the city hall and file a petition for the office of police magistrate. Emma looked at me as though she thought I was crazy. It was kind of an unheard-of thing to do, and the more I thought about it, the more I thought it was crazy, too. We discussed it further, and she told me to go ahead and continue to apply for jobs and to file for office, too. So, with her support, I knew I wanted to try.

I didn't go into politics just for personal reasons or personal gain. I really wanted to become the police magistrate so that I could work for the recovery of alcoholics. I knew how hard it was going to be in Alliance. I went to the city clerk's office and told the city clerk I wanted to file as a candidate for police magistrate. The lady said that to qualify to be on the ballot I had to be a registered voter and a resident of the city for six months. So, that day I registered to vote. Emma also registered. After I registered, I went back to the city clerk's office and filed as a candidate for police magistrate. The clerk gave me a petition and told me that I had to have 300 registered voters sign this petition and to bring the petition back to her. She would check and see if the people were valid voters. If they were, she would notarize the petition, and my name would be placed on the ballot. I knew some people in Alliance, but I didn't think I knew 300 registered voters. That night the Alliance *Times Herald* reported that Mark Monroe had filed for the office of police magistrate, and this news certainly upset our Alliance citizens. The editor or publisher of our paper made a big story of it, and it sounded like a Ripley's "Believe It or Not" type of thing. In the long run, it may have helped me. The same day that I got the petition, I called a few of my friends and asked them if they'd sign it. They did, and I began to get signatures by going from house to house. These were all white people, and 150 of them signed.

Every Indian I asked couldn't sign, however, because he wasn't registered to vote. So I went to my mother-in-law's place and to all of my Indian friends' homes and asked them, "Aren't you guys registered to vote?" I talked to all the people and told them I had gone down and registered to vote. "I'm running for police magistrate," I said, "and I want you guys to vote for me and get me elected." So all my Indian friends started questioning me, and I think some were kind of scared to go to the county clerk's office to get registered. My mother-in-law and father-in-law and my mother and father went there with them. In about four or five days after all this work, I must have gotten at least 90 people registered to vote for the first time in their lives.

About two or three days before the time limit was up on my petition, I still needed 45 or 50 more signatures. The media got hold of the story, and they followed up on what I was doing. This helped me. It gave me a lot of leeway, such

as going into the police station. I knew that the city jail always had ten of our local winos in there and that none of
them were registered to vote, either. That morning there were
twelve guys in jail, so I asked the chief of police if I could
go talk to them, and he said to go ahead. I went in, talked,
and asked them if they were registered to vote. They said,
"What's that? What do we do?" I told them I was going to
run for the lady's job of police magistrate who had put them
in there. "I'm running against her," I said, "and I need registered voters. If I can get you up to the county clerk's office
and have you registered, would you do it?" They all said, yes,
they would register and vote for me.

The next morning I took five guys up to the county
clerk's office from the city jail with the chief of police's permission. He kind of supported me and liked the fact that an
Indian was finally doing something. When I think back to
that morning, I always remember Stanley Standing Soldier,
who was a very good friend of mine and one of my former
drinking partners, a gutter-type wino. Stanley was in the
Navy, and he was a very intelligent person, but he was
hooked on wine. Stanley never became physically violent or
mentally ill. He was one of the winos who is still drinking today. He was a very comical type of guy, always joking and
raising heck with somebody.

When I took the five guys up to the county clerk's office, Stanley was the first in line. He signed his name and put
down everything but an address. The county clerk looked at
it, and she said, "Mr. Standing Soldier, what is your address
because I've got to go by the address to decide what ward
you should vote in?" He looked at her and said, "My address
is the Alliance City Jail." The county clerk said, "No, you've
got to have an address." Stanley looked at me. He was the
type of guy who lived in a park or in abandoned cars, anywhere he could find a place to drink. So he didn't have an
address. Stanley said he had been in jail twenty times a year
and spent all his time in there. The jail was some place to eat

and some place to sleep. The police needed someone to work free of charge on the garbage truck.

The county clerk looked at me and said, "Mark, is this guy for real?" I said, "You bet." Stanley had lived in Alliance ever since I could remember. He came here in 1941, the same time my mother and dad did, but he didn't have an address. However, he was and is a resident of Alliance. The county clerk couldn't believe it. She said, "I didn't know people like Stanley existed here. I thought everybody had an address." Very hesitantly, she took down Stanley Standing Soldier's address as the Alliance City Jail.

I think what was happening now was that the city of Alliance and its problem with Indian alcoholism was finally coming into focus. Some of the people in Alliance didn't even know we had that many alcoholics who didn't have a residence and couldn't give a street number address and who didn't have any place to live. I'm glad this happened because I found out later on that members of the news media were following me around town to find out whether I was putting out enough effort and initiative to get on the ballot. A lot of people were watching me closely.

I worked all day and clear into the night sometimes, trying to get the still-needed names on this petition of mine. I was still short and had only a couple of days left to get it in. One night, I attended a couple of AA meetings in Alliance, and I took my petition along with me. The AA meeting was full of rich white people who didn't want anything to do with an Indian. So when I went in and asked some of the members to sign the petition, they absolutely wouldn't do it.

I still needed some signatures on my petition, and I thought at this time maybe I'd exhausted all my supply of names and people that I knew. What I did next was to go into a bar. I knew all these guys were drinking, and I knew the bartender. The people who were there all seemed to like me. I asked the bartender or the owner if I could give a little speech. He quieted everybody down, and then I told them,

"My name is Mark Monroe, and I filed for police magistrate. I want to get on the ballot, and I need your signature on my petition if you are registered." So, in King's Corner Bar, people just came up to me saying, "Mark, you really want to get that old lady out of there?" They were really talking bad about Mrs. Johnstone. I told them I did, and a lot of them signed.

So I went from bar to bar in Alliance until I had my petition filled with 375 signatures. I wanted to get on that ballot so badly that sometimes I worked clear up until the bars closed. I wanted to get more than 300 signatures, at least 400 if possible, in case some of the names were rejected. In this two-week period I worked so hard and I knew I was still weak, but just the fact that I had a chance and had the support of these people who signed their names and were registered made me very happy. I was very proud of my mother and father, my mother-in-law and father-in-law, who finally were going to vote, and all these guys from the city jail.

A lot of people made fun of me, and a lot of them supported me, and a lot ran me into the ground thinking Indians shouldn't do this kind of thing. "It's unheard of—What are you going to do when you get in there? You don't have enough education, and you aren't qualified for this job." These were the comments I heard. But I did get 90 or more Indian people registered to vote. I'm pretty proud of that fact. This was the first time the city of Alliance had Indian people come to the county clerk's office to register to vote. Our Alliance *Times Herald* and our radio in Alliance (we didn't have a TV station at that time), these two news media covered all I had done. They even mentioned my taking American Indians from the jail and registering them with city jail as their address. Everybody was waiting to see if I could get 300 registered voters' names and be on the ballot.

In the end, I got nearly 400 signatures, and a lot of Indian people registered for the first time. People were voicing their concern in the Alliance *Times Herald*'s "Rumblings" col-

umn. They would say that an Indian is running for public office—congratulate him and support him. In a two-week period I made a big step forward for our Indian people, and I
didn't know that this kind of support existed. I could look in
Emma's eyes and know she was very proud that I even tried.
My children were elated. There were so many positive things
coming out of this experience, and it was something that I
should have done years ago. That's the way I was feeling at
that time.

It was on Friday evening. My petition was due at five
o'clock when the city clerk's office closed. I walked up there
with this petition, and when I went into her office, reporters
from our radio station and the Alliance *Times Herald* were
there, standing around waiting for me to make this deadline.
At this point in my life, I was beginning to understand politics and how to fight back against the opposition. Even
though I had my petition ready that morning, I didn't want
to go down there and just give it to them. Instead, I knew the
longer I waited, the more newsworthy it would be. This was
what I wanted, to be on the news. I was getting smart. So I
waited.

I think I waited until about a quarter to five. It was
very shortly before the office closed. I went up to the city
clerk and said, "Here's my petition; will you accept it?" And
she had to get a notary public and sign in exactly the time
I entered my petition. When I did this, the news reporter
started asking me questions right away. I told him right then
and there that I was running for the office of police magistrate for these reasons, and when I had told the public, they
were happy to sign my petition. The night I filed my petition,
I got the news coverage that really helped me later in my
campaign for the police magistrate's office. The city clerk told
me that Monday morning they would have to go through all
the names and verify that they were all registered voters. She
told me that by Monday or Tuesday I would be notified
whether I would be on the ballot for election or not.

That weekend, I think, was one of the busiest week-ends I ever had. A lot of people who didn't believe that an Indian person could ever do this—because nothing like this ever happened before—called and told us how happy they were. A lot of my Indian friends came over to our house to congratulate me and my family, because everybody knew what Emma had gone through during this drinking period of mine, and I think they were very happy and proud of my family and me.

Someone knocked at the door, and there was old John Anderson standing there, one of the most respected members in our community. I was very surprised. As the county attor-ney he had helped put me into Fort Meade many years ago, and he had now gone into private practice. He had always been a pretty good buddy of mine. John asked me how I was and how I was doing, and he seemed very happy that I was sober. It had been a long time since John had seen me that way. Evidently, he had been reading the paper and following what I had been trying to do. We sat there drinking a cup of coffee, and he asked me if I knew what to do as a police magistrate, if I knew what the job involves and some of the court procedure and the laws that you follow. I told him, "Hell, no, I don't know nothing about it, but I want to learn."

He said there was a lot involved. Every afternoon from now on, he said, at three o'clock I should come to his home, and he would teach me some of the things that a police mag-istrate would have to do according to law. He said the way he saw things, I stood a pretty good chance of getting elected, and he wanted me to go into that office knowing the job. This really surprised me. I didn't think that my filing for pub-lic office would ever create this kind of awareness or atten-tion from people like John Anderson. I told John I wanted to run and to tell me where he lived, and I'd be over there at three o'clock. After that, I always made my time clear at three o'clock so I'd go to John's home from three to five-thirty or six every evening for the rest of the time until the election.

John started teaching me the things that a judge had to know and some of the things that a judge had to do. One of the things that I did not know was that Mrs. Johnstone was a police magistrate and also the county judge, too. She held both of her courts in the same building. John told me, "Mark, if you win the police magistrate job, you'll have to tell Mrs. Johnstone to move her county job into the county building. This is perfectly right; if you win the judgeship, you have the right to do this." Without John Anderson's help, if I'd won the election, I would have been very afraid and maybe even run out of office. But John did this for me, and I've always been grateful for that man, because he did help me, and I did learn a lot about city and county laws.

Newspapers across the whole state took our *Times Herald* stories and printed them, so my campaign became statewide news. I didn't ever think that my being on the ballot would create the type of concern and awareness that it did or the quarrels it caused among the white people. Some of them were supporting me, and others weren't. It was just a really controversial thing here in Alliance.

Monday evening, the city clerk called me to her office. I went down there, and they verified pretty near every one of the signatures I had on my petition. The media was there again and told the story. The newspaper printed, "Monroe will appear on the ballot as a candidate for police magistrate." It went on to tell some of my life history as an American Indian and that I was the first American Indian to ever file for public office. It created so much news here in Alliance that at times I was kind of afraid to go around. Sometimes during the night, we'd get crank phone calls from people who'd call us all kinds of names. For a while it became very dangerous for my children. Terry, Daryl, and Connie were going to school at that time, and some white parents didn't like the idea that I was running. It caused a lot of fights between the children. Practically every morning after I found out I was going to be on the ballot, our sidewalk would be covered with eggs, and on the front of our house they'd hang dirty signs on the walls and scrawl more stuff over our front steps. I saw things like this happen on TV and thought it was a hardship for my family, but it was something we had to go through.

One day, Mrs. Lewis, a very close friend living across the street from us, called me up and asked if she could send a very good friend of hers over to meet me, and I told her I would talk to him. This was probably in February or March of 1969. Kenneth Lincoln came to our door and introduced himself to me. He had lived here in Alliance most of his life, and I had read about Ken in the paper quite often. He was a good athlete and a good golfer. Ken was really a nice appearing man, very well educated, and very interested in my running for police magistrate. After we talked for quite some time, I was really surprised that someone like Ken was so interested in my electioneering, you might say. But Ken started writing articles in the paper for me, and my election really seemed to be going well. He helped me all the way through the campaign, and I think he was kind of surprised that I didn't win because everything seemed to be going good for us.

The primary election was held in early May, and I did lose, but some of the things that happened to me in that interim period were really comical. Ken did a lot of writing about how it was the first time that an Indian ever ran for public office. He said people should support the fact that a Native American was running for police magistrate.

Ken wrote a letter to the editor of the Alliance *Times Herald* that was published a few days before the election. He said he thought there were some important steps for Alliance to take if it wanted to help its Indian population, starting with electing me as police magistrate. There should be a ward for Indian patients at St. Joseph's Hospital, and Indians should be allowed to serve on our local police force. The high school had to graduate Indian students, which it had never done before, and there needed to be an Indian counselor appointed to the school board. He wanted to show that it was possible for people of different races to get along in Alliance. The community would be strengthened by this kind of effort.

When I first filed for public office, there were two other people running for the police magistrate job: Mrs. Johnstone and a man who used to work at the meat market where we shopped. But during the time that Ken was doing all the writing and I was getting very popular in Alliance, this man suddenly disappeared, and I started to ask around town what happened to him. Someone told me he became so frustrated over running for police magistrate, since I had also entered the picture as a candidate, that it must have gotten to him. I was told he was sent to a mental institution. With Ken's help, with the attorney's help, and with a lot of friends in town backing me, we were getting a lot of good publicity. I never spent a dime for promotion, but I had more publicity than the other candidates.

During this time, I was also invited to the Elks Club to speak at a symposium that was held for the candidates. When I was told about being invited to go there to give my views about the job and about the police magistrate's office, I was very surprised because at that time Indian people weren't even allowed in the Elks Club. It's still that way today. When the man approached me about speaking there, I told him right away that I could not go into the Elks Club because I'm an Indian, and the Elks charter says that it's for Caucasian people only. He didn't know that the Elks didn't allow Indian people into their club, but he said he'd make arrangements to have me allowed in. But I didn't feel comfortable in that situation and didn't want to go into that racist club. I also thought it could be dangerous. When Ken found out about this, he supported me, but he said I'd better go and present my views. Finally, I made up my mind that I would go. I think the only reason they had that symposium was to picture me in a negative light.

Everybody had to wear ties and suits to make a good appearance. But I didn't have any suitable clothes. On the day of the symposium I met a friend of mine uptown. His name was Larry Lassick, and he was a social welfare director at that time. He asked me how I was going to dress. I told him, "I'll just have to go in my shirt and the way I dress normally because I don't have anything better to wear." Well, he wanted me to have a tie and look good. That afternoon he took me and bought me a shirt, tie, sweater, and new pants. A lot of people went out of their way and did a lot for me during this time, because probably they wanted to see an Indian win and, if he was elected, just what he would do when he got into office.

That night I did go to the Elks Club, was admitted, and was treated very nicely. Everybody there seemed to be pretty decent. I knew if I didn't appear, this would go against me in the election. I'm glad I did because after what happened at the Elks Club, I drew a lot of votes. I changed a lot of peoples' minds, particularly the ones who were rich and who were the establishment in Alliance. We had three men who were moderators for the program. I was told I would speak with Mrs. Johnstone. Then they would ask questions first of Mrs. Johnstone, then of me.

She answered a lot of questions. Some asked how much her salary was, but Mrs. Johnstone didn't want to tell anybody that, so she said, "Well, I make less than the dog-catcher here in Alliance." Unfortunately for her, the dog-catcher or animal control officer was sitting right in the front row, and he stood right up and cussed her out. He said, "Don't you ever compare your job to mine. I work hard." He told her off, and it really made her look bad. Mrs. Johnstone had been in office for twenty-five years, but she sure didn't present herself well that night. She wouldn't answer very many of the questions that were given to her from the audience either. She was very prim and proper, and with her college education, she knew that I didn't stand much of a chance against her, so she didn't put up too much of a fight.

When it came my time for questions, I was really nervous. I knew that a lot of people in the crowd of maybe 100 or 150 people were all white, rich, establishment people, and I thought they were going to really rake me over the coals. When I got up, I introduced myself. "My name is Mark Monroe. I have lived in Alliance since 1941. I am an alcoholic, but I haven't had a drink for six months." This is what the attorney told me to say about my being an alcoholic. I think the reason for that was, he told me, "Well, how many people in the audience can say they haven't had a drink for six months?" He said probably none of them could answer that, but my saying so would get over the fact that I was an alcoholic who just got out of the treatment center. It would stop a lot of people from asking more questions about it. Well, it did. Some people clapped for me who were probably alcoholics or had drinking problems. It made me feel good.

One of the questions was about my education. I told them that I had nine years of formal education and that what else I know I learned through experience in life. Another guy asked about my qualifications for running for public office, for the police magistrate's job. I told him my qualifications were that I had been in front of Mrs. Johnstone as prisoner and the only thing she ever said was, "Are you guilty, or not guilty?" Usually I was guilty, so I'd plead guilty, and the only thing she ever did was to fine me fifteen dollars, and, I said, *I can do that*. I told the man I thought my qualification was that I could do the job. I don't know whether this made a lot of people mad or not because nobody said a word for a long, long time. Finally, one man got up and started clapping for me. In comparison with Mrs. Johnstone, I was speaking the truth and telling people what I wanted to do and that I would do something about it. This really fouled up Mrs. Johnstone's image right then and there.

I told them also, being an Indian alcoholic, I would work with Indian alcoholics and try to promote programs to help sober them up. I said this had never been done before. In the twenty-five years that Mrs. Johnstone had been magistrate, no attempt had ever been made to work with Indian or non-Indian alcoholics. It was just the swinging-door type of thing where you go in, get fined, and if you can't pay your fine, you go to work with the city trash truck. No attempt was ever made to help these people. We, at that time, had the highest arrest record for intoxication anywhere in the state of Nebraska. I told them that after I fined a man and sentenced him, I would try to do something for him. This seemed to please the crowd very much. Some of the people who I was very afraid might do me a lot of harm stood up and started clapping. Because I was speaking the honest truth, it probably brought me a lot of votes.

At that time, I was getting statistics on how many Indian alcoholics went through city jail. At one time, there were 150 different men who had gone before Mrs. Johnstone, and practically every one of them was an Indian. Stanley Standing Soldier had been in jail twenty times in one year. I got these statistics from the county clerk's office. I also told the crowd at the Elks about Stanley. I said, "Now, here is a man who has been in jail twenty times, and he's never been offered any type of recovery program. It has been just an ongoing type of swinging-door thing for him, and he's the kind of man I want to do something for. After I fined him, sentenced him, I would try to rehabilitate him because right now all we're doing is just playing games with this guy."

Everything seemed to be going real well. After the crowd in the Elks Club started supporting me, I found out I could talk a lot better than I thought and could get my viewpoints across. I think that after what Mrs. Johnstone tried to do and what she said, the crowd became very negative toward her. They didn't want to ask her any more questions. She represented the institution type of people we had here in town, and she didn't want to change. She didn't want to do anything progressive. After the symposium was over, I answered every question that was given to me the best I could and honestly. I think I made a lot of friends in the Elks Club that night. I was asked by some of the people to become a member of the club. But with my own feelings so strong, I politely turned them down. I simply said, "No, I don't want to be a member of the Elks Club, but I thank you very much for letting me speak at your symposium." And that was it. I came out of there feeling happy just over the fact that I had gone and spoken to them.

The next day Mr. Kemper, the editor or publisher of our local paper, wrote a big story about the event, but he didn't report that the crowd accepted me well and cheered me on. He has died since then, but his son runs the Alliance *Times Herald* now, and we still have the very same thing. He is an establishment person, and whatever he doesn't like, he won't print in the paper. Of course, a lot of people listen to him. Even though I got my points across positively and truthfully, it still didn't sound right when it came out in the paper. This made Ken mad because he was at that symposium, too, and heard everything that was said. He knew about the people supporting me. So Ken started writing editorials in the paper again, and some of the editorials that he wrote kind of made Mr. Kemper look bad. Anyway, as far as I was concerned, I was feeling good about the election.

At this time Emma was working for Dr. Goding, a dentist here in town. She worked for his wife as a housekeeper, and Mrs. Goding really like Emma. Fact is, they were very close friends. I was told that two or three days after Ken started writing, Dr. and Mrs. Goding were having supper at one of our local restaurants. Mr. Kemper was also there and started making remarks about me and my candidacy in a very loud, coarse voice. So Dr. Goding got up from his table and went to Mr. Kemper's and told him to keep his mouth shut. He said that I had done a lot of things that need praise instead of running me down. I guess Mr. Kemper was a fighter, too, and they had an argument in the restaurant over my running for public office.

I was told later on that this was happening in the Elks Club, in the American Legion, all the veterans' clubs—that people were taking up sides for me, and there were rumors of other fistfights. I really didn't know what to think at this point. I seemed to be causing a lot of good and bad publicity. The only good thing that came out of it was that people were taking an interest. They were seeing the point of view of a Native American.

Sometimes I felt sorry I had decided to run for office, but with a lot of encouragement from Ken and from Mr. Anderson, the attorney, and the welfare officer, Larry Lassick, I just kept going. I thought I was creating a lot of hatred and division in Alliance, and it kind of made me feel bad. However, I continued going from bar to bar, where I'd talk to people and tell them what I was going to do. I was invited to several ladies' clubs to talk to them, too. I think my appearance at a lot of these places just changed a lot of peoples' minds. For many of them, their image of an American Indian in Alliance was the "dirty, lazy, drunk" stereotype. A lot of these people were really surprised when I'd show up in good clothes, sober, and they gave me a lot of moral support so I was able to get my views across to them.

As I mentioned, I had also applied for the job as director of our Community Action Center. I knew I could do it because even though I'd had only nine years of formal education, I was good at bookkeeping. Sometime in February or March, they interviewed me for the job. There was one other Indian who applied, Carl Janis, who had come from South Dakota. He was a college graduate and had had a lot of experience in directing on the reservation. I thought that Carl would probably get the job because he had more experience than I did.

When I went for the interview, I told them about my

being an alcoholic, of course, but I didn't have to tell them about running for city election because it was something everyone knew and was talking about in Alliance. The man who was doing the hiring called me up one afternoon and said that I did not get the job, but the only reason I was turned down was because Mr. Janis had more education. He was very nice about it, so I accepted it.

About the same time, I was contacted by Mark Goldfuss, a VISTA worker. He called me about a job opening with the Panhandle Mental Health Center in Scottsbluff. He wanted me to apply for it because the job was working with Indian alcoholics and Indian mental patients. So I did, and I talked to the mental health representative who seemed to be very interested in me. I was on my way again.

After Mr. Carl Janis got the job at the Community Action Center, I used to go there quite often at night. I knew Community Action was good for the city of Alliance because it represented the low-income and minority people. Almost all of them were Indian. I knew after staying around the center that we needed more than just giving people food and clothing. It was the center that hired people for mainstream programs now that it was part of the Comprehensive Employment and Training Act (CETA). But I knew something else had to be added. I talked with Mr. Janis one time and said, "Let's start an Indian committee and try and get some of our rights, some of our views across to the white population here in Alliance. We need to find out why they are sending us to jail, why they are not trying to help us recover, and why there is so much racism here." He agreed and promised to support me in any way he could.

That evening I went home and wrote some kind of speech to present to people. What we were going to do was call upon the mayor, the city councilmen, the judges, the chief of police, the social services office director, and anybody who was in some kind of position in Alliance to help the American Indian. What I wrote down was an American Indian Committee philosophy. We would read this to people we invited to our meetings and question them as to why American Indians weren't receiving the recognition and the care that they deserved. I wrote that night, "We have organized an American Indian Committee. A committee of non-violence. We have no wish to violate the laws of city or state. We have no ideas of revenge. We simply want to know our rights and what could be done when these rights are violated. We feel that many of them have been violated and would like very much to have an explanation. We think that working as a group will be more effective in solving our problems."

I took my statement to Mr. Janis, and he was really happy about it. At the first meeting that we had, I was in complete control because nobody but Indian people were allowed to attend. We probably drew 125 of them. Everyone who came told me that I should have been the director of the Community Action program. I didn't like that because I didn't want to create a division between Mr. Janis and myself; I thought he was well qualified for the job and that was the way we should keep it.

During this meeting of the Indian people, I was elected chairman of the American Indian Committee. We also elected a vice-chairman and secretary. I conducted all the meetings and was the person who went out to make the invitations for public servants to attend. The first man I contacted was Glenn Fiebig, a former FBI man. He had retired in Alliance and was hired by the county as the county attorney. The county attorney was the person who would always do his best to get an Indian convicted no matter what the charge was. He was anti-Indian, you might say. However, he was the first person on the list to attend our American Indian Committee meeting. Soon as Mr. Fiebig came into our group session with about a hundred Indian people there, we questioned him to see if we could do something about his convicting so many of our people.

Well, when Mr. Fiebig came into our room, it must

have looked kind of dangerous to him. The first remark he made was, "I'm not afraid of Indian people." Everybody in the room started laughing at him. He was so uneasy. I went up to the door and told him that he was welcome at the meeting and that it shouldn't last more than a couple of hours. I made him feel at ease. We sat him down, and a lot of people started asking him questions. Some of the people were mad at him, and this was the only chance they ever had in their lives to question somebody like Mr. Fiebig. I think a lot of the questions were completely out of line and were very derogatory toward him, but I kind of fielded the questions. Whenever someone would ask an embarrassing, derogatory one, I'd stop it, and we'd go on from there. Mr. Fiebig didn't give too many explanations because he was the law in the county, and I don't think we did anything to influence any decisions he was going to make. But it turned out to be a real good session.

I believe that forming the American Indian Committee in 1969 was very effective. As a committee of people representing the American Indian in Alliance, we got a lot of recognition, and a lot of people heard about our concerns. I think we gained a lot of respect in the community, too. In our philosophy, we were not militant or planning on any revenge. All we wanted to do was to be heard, and to be recognized. I think we accomplished that. We did call about every director of every organization in Alliance. We also worked and called many of the people from the school system, like the superintendent of schools, the principals of the local elementary schools, the junior and senior high schools. At that time, American Indian children were having a lot of problems, but after we got some of these administrators to attend our meeting, things seemed to change a lot. I think what was happening in Alliance was that the American Indian was finally being recognized as a human being. Most people thought of us as second-class citizens. But when we, as parents, spoke up for our children, it seemed to draw a lot of attention, and things got done.

To give an example: One night during the same election that I was running for police magistrate, there were about four or five people running for the school board. At this meeting the five candidates were presented: Dr. Richard Jaggers, Mrs. Ray Fulton, Kenneth Dobby Lee, Jack Moldern, Terry Shannon. Most of them entered into the question-and-answer discussion that followed Mr. Johnson's report. Now, Mr. Johnson was working for the local school board. He had a master's degree in sociology from the University of Wyoming and had been working in the area since early on in the 1968–69 school year. Mr. Johnson warned that Alliance was a potential racial hot spot, that red (Indian) militants were coming in calling for Red Power. He declared that problems in school children should be identified in grade school, and that when they were identified at this early age, they could be corrected.

Mr. Johnson refused to attend our meetings, but he had the nerve to report to the school board about us. So the very same day that this story came out in the paper, we got together and gave a statement to a reporter from the *Times Herald*.

What we said was, "The Alliance American Indian Committee has read the article in the Wednesday's *Times Herald* concerning the report of an individual to the school board in regard to racial problems in Alliance. This person is totally misinformed as to the attitude of the American Indian citizens of Alliance. The statement that red militants are coming into town calling for Red Power is characteristic of his charges. We, as Indian people, know of no such red militancy. The individual in question is not considered a knowledgeable reference by Indian people. He has neither attended any meetings of the Alliance American Indian Committee, nor has he discussed its policies with its officers. In order to explain our organization to the public, we, hereby, publish our statement of philosophy concerning the formation of our organization." And we restated our philosophy and signed our names: "the American Indian Committee, Mark Monroe

Chairman, Members James Schmidt, Edward Flood, Carl Janis and Carol Janis."

The day that our reply came out in the paper, Mr. Johnson was removed from his position, and I was told that he was fired because he had falsely called the American Indians "red militants." Mr. Johnson and the school board were very fearful that we, as a committee, would bring suit against them for making statements that were completely untrue. The part I really liked about it was that the county attorney, the chief of police, the welfare director, the sheriff, and everybody we had called to our meeting supported us. We commanded a lot of respect. I didn't like the idea of Mr. Johnson losing his job, but I think it was his fault.

With my running for public office and making speeches for a number of organizations who would call our committee and ask for me, a lot of good things began to happen. The rapport between whites and Indians improved and made Alliance so much more livable for us. Our Indian children began to attend school, and the arrest record for Indian people went down quite a bit during this period. During my campaign I told people that I would ask the city council not to use Indian people who were arrested for being drunk as workers on the trash trucks. The American Indian Committee also wanted this practice stopped. Alliance got thousands and thousands of dollars per year from drunk Indian people. Word got around to the police and Mrs. Johnstone that they better not arrest Indian people unless they had a valid reason to do so.

We were gaining respect, recognition. Because of the American Indian Committee, Indian people were working together. I felt very proud of the fact that I had organized this committee, and our members were very proud, too, because, for once, we were getting something done. The American Indian Committee was still operating out of the Community Action Center in the spring of 1969. Everything was working real well, but of course, we still had a lot of flak coming from the community about why an Indian was running for public office.

During the campaign, we had a local Indian businessman by the name of Mr. Tyndall, who came to me and to the committee offering assistance. He runs Tyndall's Plumbing. Mr. Tyndall used to be a white man. Although he was Indian, he never did socialize with Indian people, and I think a lot of times he was probably ashamed that he was an Indian. But he put me on the air on radio and wrote up several articles about having an Indian candidate for police magistrate. I think my campaign really brought about a lot of Indian awareness in Alliance.

My campaign was still going well at this time. I continued to go to the attorney's home to learn the laws and how to be a police magistrate. I met a lot of important people in Alliance, and I learned a lot. Ken left Alliance sometime in March of 1969 with his wife and his daughter, Rachel, who was probably about five or six months old. After Ken left, I kind of felt bad and got scared all over again. However, I continued with the election, which wouldn't be held until May 5th. Sometimes at night I would think to myself, what if I did win? Things like that sometimes scared me. I don't really know what I would have done if I had won the police magistrate's position then. I wonder if I would have been a good judge, and if I would have been able to handle it. A lot of times when I think back about that time and how I recuperated from alcoholism and the years at Fort Meade, I'm glad these things happened to me. They made me a better person and better able to work with people. I think what I did by filing for police magistrate and forming the American Indian Committee was helpful. It got Indian people recognized, and recognition was the most important thing we accomplished. To have white people think good of us instead of always stereotyping us was a big step forward.

C•H•A•P•T•E•R IX

INDIGENOUS MENTAL
HEALTH WORKER

In the early spring of 1969, I applied for a job at the Panhandle Mental Health Center in Scottsbluff, Nebraska. One day I got a letter asking me to appear there to be interviewed by the staff. So I drove to Scottsbluff and met Dr. Allen Roehl, who was and still is the center's clinical psychologist and director. I also met with Rev. William Nisl, who was the consulting pastor, and a fellow by the name of Bob Bontrager, who was the social services director in the Mental Health Center. These three men introduced me to all the staff. I felt out of place and scared when they took me into a building where there were psychiatrists, psychologists, and social workers—all very educated people. But these fellows really made me feel at home. I thought the three of them were the people who were going to interview me about the job, but I wound up meeting in the dayroom with the whole staff—probably around twelve to fifteen people, including psychiatric nurses and all those who were doing janitorial services. I think the reason for this was because they were told, for the first time in the history of the Mental Health Center, they were going to employ an Indian. Everyone was interested. It was explained that this Indian did not have a formal high school diploma or any college degrees. Later Dr. Roehl wrote a paper about me after I was employed and said that the staff was wondering how they, as college-educated people, would respond to a man who did not have an education and how he would respond to them. Well, I felt somehow at ease and at home, so I did a real good job. I think there were two other men in Alliance who had been interviewed for this job but, somehow or another, I was chosen.

Basically the job they wanted me to do was to come back into my community and do the very same things that I had already started with the American Indian Committee, such as developing awareness of Native Americans in their indigenous homes or places. It was important not only that they would feel part of that community but that they be a help to that community as well. I think in my candidacy and also my work with the American Indian Committee that I had already done this. They already had a title for me, "Indigenous Indian Mental Health Worker."

From that day on, the only thing they would do was to direct me. They just wanted me basically to go to every Indian community in western Nebraska. We would start in communities like Gordon, Hay Springs, Chadron, Alliance, Scottsbluff, Kimball, and Sidney. My job was to go into these areas and to make the town or city aware that Indian people were living there who could become responsible citizens. Also, I was to work with Indian alcoholics and with Indian people who had mental problems.

Later on, I think the Mental Health Center was issued a court order from Lincoln, Nebraska, which is the capital of the state. Even though the Mental Health Center had been open for the past ten to fifteen years, they had never had an Indian patient voluntarily come to them for treatment. The only time that they would get an Indian there would be under court commitment. A person who is under court commitment is one for whom nothing has ever worked. As soon as the court commitment period is up, the Indian stops going.

It was generally explained to me that I should do exactly the same thing that I had done in my community but for the whole panhandle of Nebraska. The only thing they wanted me to do further was come to a staff meeting every Wednesday morning in Scottsbluff. I would tell them about my progress and how the Indian people were reacting to our mental health program and an Indian mental health worker.

When they interviewed me for the job, a lot of people,

including Dr. Roehl, wanted to know why Indian people would not go to a mental health clinic. I remembered that when I had the problem with alcoholism, I was very fearful of going to a psychiatrist or psychologist to get help. Any time a psychiatrist or a psychologist is mentioned, an Indian person immediately thinks there is something wrong with their head, either they're insane or having mental problems. In the Indian culture, any time an Indian has a mental health problem, it is so shameful to the family that they hide the problem instead of doing something about it. Many years ago, any Indian who had a mental problem or was insane was taken somewhere way out into the country, left, and forgotten. That person was disowned by the family. I always wonder if one of the reasons we have so many Indian alcoholics is the stigma that goes along with asking for services from a mental health program.

In the 1940s and 1950s we had a man here in Alliance who was a *winkte*—that's the way the Indian people say it. The way white people would say it would be he was a transvestite, as he was a man but he acted like a woman. This poor man was shunned by everyone in Alliance. Nobody wanted anything to do with him except for his mother, and she loved him dearly. So she would take him around. Even when he used to talk to me, I'd just ignore him. This Indian concern about bringing shame on the family still exists today.

When I told this to Dr. Roehl, he didn't believe it right away, but the staff did. They knew they never did have any Indian patient walk in through the door on a voluntary basis, so there had to be something wrong. They didn't know the Indian and about some of the taboos in our culture or that there are things we don't do. They never learned about Indian culture in books or in school.

One of the first things that I did was to attend the courts. I was really interested in going in order to find out how the judge handled or worked with the Native American person. I would read the paper and learn when court was in session, who was going to be there, and if there was an Indian on trial. If so, I'd go. I found out that many Indian people would just go to court where the judge or county attorney would read the complaint against him. In a lot of cases, Indians didn't understand what they were being charged with, what they had done, what their rights were or that a lawyer could be assigned to them free of charge. At this time, they didn't have the county defender, but each county was obligated to secure an attorney for any indigent person. The only thing that the American Indians were used to doing was going into court where the judge would ask, "Are you guilty?" and they'd say, "Yes." So it was very easy for the county attorney and the judge. Some cases didn't last five minutes.

I kept daily notation of what time I attended court and what the decision of the court was. After about two or three weeks of my attending, the American Indians started saying, "Look, I plead not guilty." They started defending themselves a little bit better or asking questions. Just by being in court, I may have started something good in Alliance. A lot of the Indian people didn't understand English and could just barely speak it. These were some of the things the court was failing to recognize—and it had never been brought to the attention of the judge before.

One morning when I went to court, I think the judge had become aware that I was there in his courtroom, and he realized that many of the things that were happening were not due procedure of law. This particular morning he asked me, "Mark, I have a case here where this man told me he does not understand English or he does not speak English well enough to be in court. Would you interpret for him?" So I told him, "Sure, I'll do the best I can." I did, and the case turned out real well. I can't remember this Indian's name, but he told me everything he did, and I told the judge. When the whole story came out, the man was actually not guilty.

This started something, and I became a kind of interpreter in Alliance. Whenever an Indian couldn't understand or speak English, I was called in. With every case, I'd write down what happened, and I kept a daily log of what I'd done. This got to working so well that in Sheridan County, which would be Rushville, Nebraska, I'd be called there to interpret, too. The reason they called me was that I did not charge, which the counties liked.

When I went to the staff meetings on Wednesdays and told them what I had done, it was so incredible to the staff of the Mental Health Center; they didn't know about this type of work. They all agreed that it was something that comes under the work of the mental health center and somehow it was forgotten by the psychologists and psychiatrists. We had a lot of discussions about ways to humanize people.

I was paid to be a mental health worker, but these other things were what I chose to do even though I was under no specific directions to do them. Accounts of some of the things I did with the Mental Health Center were sent on to Lincoln, where the headquarters were, and they were approved as being part of the mental health services that should be offered. As far as I was concerned, all I wanted to do was to create a humanistic approach among the Indian people so that they could speak for themselves, defend themselves, and ask for help whenever a mental health problem arose.

It worked out that just by my being in court, a lot of awareness was created on the part of the judge, the county attorney, and the prisoner. Things worked well. A lot of times a few of the county attorneys and a few of the judges called Dr. Roehl and asked him what I was doing in court. Dr. Roehl always explained to them, "I don't know. Mr. Monroe is working that area, and you'll have to ask him." So he really supported me. I wasn't violating any laws or violating anybody's rights; I was merely a spectator in court.

When I started working for the Mental Health Center in March 1969, a lot of publicity again was created in Alliance and the media were asking whether a state worker should be allowed to be a police magistrate. Dr. Roehl would respond by saying, "Mark Monroe's job is as an indigenous mental health worker, and that's what his duties are." Dr. Roehl would just cover for me, but the media would make a lot of negative remarks about my working for the state of Nebraska and still running for public office. However, the state of Nebraska had no rules that said that I couldn't do this. I was free to run for police magistrate and do anything else I wanted to as well.

During this time I still worked with the American Indian Committee and created a lot of self-help projects in Alliance for Indian people in schools and on their jobs. Attending court and learning court procedures was one of these projects.

On election day—May 5, 1969—I knew that the results could probably come in about 1:00 A.M. That night my family—Emma, Terry, Connie, Daryl, Kandi, Hope, and I—were all sitting by the radio listening for the election returns. I wanted to win very badly, but I was also afraid to win, so it was kind of a dilemma. I knew if I won, I could handle the job because of the tutoring Mr. John Anderson, the attorney, had given me and also because of the support I had from so many of the people in Alliance. Whenever I'd look at my family and know that they'd gone through hell during this campaign, I wanted to win for them. I also wanted to win in order to bring awareness of the American Indian to Alliance and in some way help them.

From about nine o'clock on that evening, I was far ahead of Mrs. Johnstone. There were about twelve wards in Alliance, and already the results from about six or seven wards had come in. It looked pretty good. Emma and the kids were all happy. About ten o'clock Mr. Anderson and Mr. Lassick came to listen with us. Although the guys were congratulating me already, it was too early. About twelve o'clock the results from Mrs. Johnstone's ward came in, and she defeated me badly. Because that ward voted 100 percent in her favor, she won the election. The radio broadcaster said that this was the closest election ever held for the police magistrate's office in years and that Mark Monroe, an American Indian, had come closer to beating Mrs. Johnstone than any of her former opponents in over twenty-five years.

When the election was over and I knew Mrs. Johnstone had won, I was relieved it was over but very proud of myself. My family was proud too. I had tried very hard, and though I didn't succeed, the Indian people in Alliance for once in their lives had drawn some attention.

The next morning when I woke up, I knew that I had to go and talk to Mrs. Johnstone and congratulate her on her victory. During the campaign I never did say anything bad about her. I think Mrs. Johnstone hurt herself by not answering the questions at the Elks symposium. I was hoping that she wouldn't be mad or hold any ill feelings toward me. However, that morning I didn't seem to care. When I went in, I started talking and said to her, "Congratulations on your victory. I'm very glad you won." She looked at me, got up off her chair, pushed it away from her bench, and came down and hugged me. When she came close, I could see tears in her eyes. When I saw that, I felt she was a good lady. I had always respected her a lot, but I don't think I really liked her. Now I began to hope she would try to understand and help the Indian people.

Next to her was seated the chief of police. In the past he and I never did get along because whenever I saw him I was either going in or out of jail; I was always drunk. However, now the chief of police stood up, shook my hand, patted me on the back, and congratulated me. Right away, I knew that I had done the right thing by going in and talking to Mrs. Johnstone and offering her my congratulations. That day I was so happy. I knew I had done something positive for the progress of the American Indian in Alliance. I also was aware that this type of thing had never happened before, and

I was the one who had done it. My running for police magistrate in Alliance created a lot of awareness of Indian people, and as a result a lot of white people changed their opinions. More Indian people were able to get work and were given a chance to prove themselves. It also stopped the arrests of Indian people for work purposes like garbage collection. In fact, the city of Alliance began hiring Indian people and putting them on salary to haul trash. A lot of good came out of the election, and I was proud of my family for supporting me, proud of all my friends—my adopted brother Ken Lincoln, Larry Lassick, John Anderson—these men, and many others like them. I just felt good.

After the election was over with, I continued to work with the Panhandle Mental Health Center, as I didn't want the momentum that I had created to end. I wanted to start more programs for Indian people, and I was now in the position to do it. All I needed was a lot of support from the Indian community. By this time I was working with many low-income people: white people, Mexican people, and a few black people who were in town. In my job for the Mental Health Center I was sent to a lot of their homes, as they did not know how to contact the Mental Health Center. These people's names were given to me—so I eventually worked with about every minority person in Alliance.

The American Indian Committee was still very active and still meeting in the Community Action Center. Community Action was an arm of the Office of Economic Opportunity, which worked with low-income people, mostly giving them commodities and money. One day Mr. Janis asked me if we could hold our committee meetings elsewhere. I think the reason was that low-income people in Alliance were getting so much publicity because of my campaign for police magistrate's office and my being employed by the Mental Health Center, and the Community Action office was afraid they might not be doing the right type of thing. They were providing direct services, which I don't oppose, but I don't think they ever took into consideration the larger aspect of helping people—mainly the motivation for becoming human beings, for trying to defend themselves, or just for becoming a person. I think, when you are working with people, you not only want to feed them and help them, but you want to do more for them as well. That's what the committee and I were trying to do.

I didn't know exactly what to do to get a building in which to hold our meetings and bingo games. We held one more meeting at the center, and I asked the members whether they wanted to continue doing what we had started. If they didn't, well, I was figuring on just ending the committee. But they wanted to continue the meetings indefinitely, and I was appointed to look for another building for us.

I thought we could use a large barracks that had been brought from the air base and placed in South Alliance in 1950. The Church Women United had bought the building and called it the Indian Social Center, where Indian people could go and hold their dances and bingo games. Somehow or other in the latter 1950s the Church Women United quit sponsoring the program, so they just closed the center, and the city of Alliance condemned the building. I contacted the city council and asked if they would lease this building to the American Indian Committee. They had already made plans to tear the building down and move it away. I told city council that we would renovate the building, bring it up to city codes, take care of it, and that we would move into it. The building even had an apartment where a family could live. The city council decided the very same night to lease it to us for one dollar a year.

Within a week's time I got some of our Indian people together as volunteers, and we went and looked at the building. It was in very bad shape. All the windows were broken, and many of the walls were damaged where someone had poked holes into them. I figured it would take maybe $1,000 to $1,500 to renovate the building. First, I got some windows from a friend of mine, then some boards and plasterboard, fixed all the walls and put in the windows, painted, and repaired the roof to make it livable. On June 1, 1969, my family and I moved into the building. Half the building was for living quarters and the other half was for meeting purposes and bingo games. Right away we started holding our meetings.

The fact is, the meetings became so interesting that a lot of the local white people asked us if they could attend. The meetings were held weekly and were about how American Indians and the white people could work together for the betterment of Alliance. A lot of the white people would come and offer suggestions, for example, about how they managed to keep their children in school, and then the Indian people would give theirs. It was just sort of a social type atmosphere, and it really worked.

The meetings got so well known that a social worker, Tom Leemy, from Hastings, Nebraska, about 350 miles from Alliance, made it a point to come every month. I haven't seen Tom since 1972 or 1973, but one time he told me that these were the best social action meetings he had ever attended. He said he learned more from hearing these people talking than he had learned all the time he was going to school. Every month he and his secretary would come and tape the meetings. I suppose they used the suggestions of the interracial interaction group. Indians and white people had a lot of suggestions about what to do, how to do it, where to do it, and when. As a mental health worker, I listened to all these suggestions and learned a lot myself.

One night at one of our meetings, many of the Alliance Indian people were telling that even when sick, if they went to a clinic, the doctor would not see them. They'd just wait and wait and wait. In one instance, a young man who was my first cousin died on the way to Hastings because a local doctor wouldn't see him. After everybody talked about it, I came up with the idea that I would go talk to the local doc-

tors' association and find out why doctors were not seeing
our Indian patients. We knew before I even went in that this
was happening because of the racial and monetary barriers.
Indians never did have money to pay for their medical visits.
Mr. Leemy, who really supported our group, told me that
whenever a sick person went to a doctor, it was the doctor's
duty to see this patient whether he had money or not. That
kind of gave me a little leverage, you might say, and initiative
to contact the physicians.

During the meeting the people again appointed me to
arrange an appointment with the County Medical Association, which included all the doctors in Alliance and Heming-
ford. I was supposed to find out if there was any kind of
arrangement that could be made so that they would see not
only Indian people, but low-income whites, Mexicans, and
blacks. When I went to Scottsbluff the next Wednesday for a
staff meeting, I brought this matter up among the staff and
told them what I planned to do. Everybody thought it was a
good idea, although they were kind of fearful about the reaction of the doctors and what they would say. I was the one
who had to do it. My first cousin's death gave me even more
initiative to see what could be done.

About a week later I talked to my personal doctor, Dr.
Robert Morgan, here in Alliance. He had helped me all
through my alcoholic years and was a very good friend of
mine. One time I asked him if he would arrange for me to attend one of their monthly meetings. He called me back and
said I was on the agenda for the meeting at the Drake Hotel,
a real fancy, high-class place where only rich white people
ate. I started getting that scared feeling back again, but the
night of the meeting I think I prepared myself very well.
There were probably twenty to twenty-five doctors present,
and they were pretty nice fellows. They even invited me to a
steak supper.

When the meeting was over with, I presented my program. I told them that they were not seeing American Indian

people at their offices and therefore many of our people were
dying. I said, "I know of one documented case where my first
cousin died because a physician wouldn't see him." I added,
"I have people who could come here right now and tell you
themselves when they were turned away by a doctor." What
we wanted to know was why this was happening. As Indian
people, we do get sick, but we are too far away from the reservation to get help, so we need to see a local doctor when
we are ill.

They were very serious, dedicated people. They sat
back and listened to what I said. When I got through giving
my presentation, one of them spoke up. He was Dr. Kennedy,
a well-known doctor here in Alliance. I'd always liked him
and known him for many years. He said that he had never
turned a patient away, but he wondered whether his receptionist had. Many of the other doctors agreed with him. I got
to thinking, maybe there is something wrong here; maybe I'm
presenting this to the wrong group of people. The doctors
said they wanted me to come back to meet in another month,
and they would go back to their clinics and find out how
many people have been turned away, who did it, why, when,
how, where, whatever, and report back at the next meeting.

When they reported back, all the doctors agreed again
that they had never turned anybody away, Indian, black,
Mexican, or white. What had happened in each clinic is that
the receptionist at the front desk, when she sees an Indian
come in and she doesn't know if he has money or not, won't
let him see the doctor. The patient feels guilty and unwanted.
Of course, with all the other white people sitting in the clinic,
the Indian patient just gives up and walks out, no matter if
he is near death or not.

Prior to my going to this meeting with the doctors
where this statement was made, I had contacted the chamber
of commerce director, Lou Flowers, who was a pretty good
friend of mine. He was new to this area, but he was very upset about the doctors not seeing Indian, Mexican, and black

people and providing them with medical service. Mr. Flowers became involved in trying to get medical help for minority people in Alliance, as he had attended some of our meetings at the American Indian Center (the name given our committee headquarters). That night at the doctor's meeting they came to a conclusion that we needed to screen patients at our center. If any minority, indigent person would need medical help, they should first go to the center and tell me. Then, I would call the doctor's clinic of their choice, and he would see this patient free of charge.

Mr. Flowers agreed to print us up some statements. We called them medical screening forms. On this form we asked the name, address, age, and sex. The doctors said they would start at the earliest date we wanted. So a week or two later I reported back at our meeting what the doctors had agreed upon. The best part about this medical screening program was that people coming through our center would be given priority. For instance, if an Indian, Mexican, black, or a low-income white person would come in, I would provide a ride for him or her, and when that person would present this medical screening form to the receptionist, she would then take the patient directly to the doctor. This seemed like a godsend for all of us. This was what the doctors wanted to arrange, and, as long as Mr. Flowers and I did what we were supposed to do, our low-income people would receive free medical attention. When I reported this, everyone seemed happy, and we got our medical screening program into operation just as soon as possible.

The first patient we sent to the clinic went to see Dr. Gardner. This patient went in on May 12, 1970, and the volunteer who did this for the patient was my wife, Emma Monroe. Our last patient was seen on March 19, 1976. This program worked wonderfully. Word got around areas such as Chadron, Gordon, Scottsbluff, and Kimball that we had started a program for free medical services for indigent people. I think on the following Wednesday when I attended the staff meeting at the Scottsbluff Panhandle Mental Health Center, I brought this to the attention of the staff and told them how we created this program, what we had done, where the meetings were held, what the wants and needs of low-income people were, how I attended the doctors' meetings, and right up to when we sent our first patient.

Well, the staff at the Mental Health Center was really questioning how this could occur, because the things that we were doing were the first time that anything like this had ever happened. It was unheard of. When our staff started discussing the medical screening program and its operation, Dr. Roehl appointed his psychiatrist and one of his psychiatric nurses to come to Alliance and see how our program was operating. This was on May 15. We had a patient we sent to Dr. Wilkinson free of charge, and we accompanied him. I drove the car, took the patient, the psychiatrist, and the psychiatric nurse right along with us. We went into the clinic, and the patient with his medical screening form from the American Indian Center was taken immediately to see the doctor, even though there were nine or ten other people sitting in the waiting room. This convinced the mental health people that the program was going to work properly. I think they were amazed.

The program kind of made me popular at the Mental Health Center as I had helped start something completely new in northwest Nebraska. Not only the Mental Health Center, but some of the staff of the Community Action program, which was headquartered in Chadron, Nebraska, also made an appointment with me in Alliance. They came and wanted to know how this medical screening program was initiated, and if I would be able to go to Chadron to speak to their doctors' association, to see if we could get a similar program started there. This happened not only in Chadron, but also in Gordon; both towns are adjacent to the Pine Ridge Reservation and have large numbers of Indian people. The Community Action staff asked me if I would go ahead and see if I could start a program for those two areas.

Prior to this time I had done a lot of work in Gordon and Chadron with Indian alcoholics, and I was acquainted with a number of Indian people. Their situation was just as bad as or worse than those who lived in Alliance. I told the Community Action people that I would have to talk with my supervisor. On the following Wednesday I brought their request to the staff. They all agreed that I should do it because what we had started with the medical screening program was already successful and something the doctors were in favor of and were happy to provide.

So with the okay of the Mental Health Center, I made arrangements with the Sheridan and Dawes County Doctors' Association, in Chadron, which is approximately sixty miles from Alliance. They met every month. Through Dr. Morgan I was introduced to one of the doctors from these two counties. We talked over the phone. I asked him whether I could attend their medical association meeting to present this program to them. I told him what had happened in Alliance, and I think he probably had heard about it through the grapevine. He was very glad to do it.

On the night of the meeting, Emma and I drove to Chadron, where the doctors were meeting in a large restaurant. When Emma and I walked in, we could hear them eating supper, joking, and having a good time. One of the doctors stood up right away and came over to us and invited us to supper. I never met this man before in my life, but right away assumed that they were very good men, the same as the doctors in Alliance. I felt very comfortable; so did Emma. But we had already eaten, so we waited until they got through. Emma and I were in a waiting room part of the restaurant when a waitress came out and said, "Dr. Monroe, the doctors are ready for you now." Emma gave me a big smile, and I smiled at her. We were dressed up pretty good and the waitress assumed that I was a doctor ready to talk to the others.

When I went in, I felt so good that I gave the doctors a good presentation of the program. I told of the success we were having getting minority people in to see the doctors and exactly how the program worked. So they discussed it for ten or fifteen minutes and right away they agreed to see the patients as long as they had a form stating that they were indigent. I thought, this thing is really catching on. This program in Sheridan and Dawes counties would cover two counties and approximately three hundred miles of area. It would cover Gordon, Rushville, Hay Springs, Chadron, and Crawford, Nebraska—five small towns on Highway 20, adjacent to the South Dakota border. I said, "Thank you," wished them well, and left.

My job after that was to go to these five little towns and make arrangements there with these medical screening forms and tell them what had happened. Everything looked real good. I got the okay from the chairman of the medical board. I was willing to do the work, but the only thing I needed then was to go to Scottsbluff and see if I could get some monetary help from them to print up some forms and get some of my mileage paid for. I knew I would have to spend a week or maybe two weeks in the area setting up these programs.

On a Wednesday morning at our staff meeting at Scottsbluff, I brought the fact up that the Sheridan and Dawes counties' doctors' association had agreed to do the very same thing we did in our county. Dr. Roehl was so pleased that he told me that whatever this program cost, he'd pay for it. The only thing I had to do is go and set them up. Of course, one of the primary jobs at the Mental Health Center was community mental health, and we were providing the services they should have been doing.

So Dr. Roehl's okay gave me the blessing, you might say. I went to each one of the Community Action offices in these towns and set up the program. The community of Gordon was also very helpful. They had forms printed up, got the program started, and it worked very efficiently. They got many low-income people to the doctor without any charge.

This happened also in Rushville. Hay Springs was such a small community that I don't think we ever got anything started there, but Chadron and Crawford had a good medical screening program. I made it a point to check on these at least every two weeks or every month. All ran very smoothly.

In our weekly meetings in Scottsbluff there were reports about how well our screening program worked. We had created a program in western Nebraska that was very helpful and completely new. Later on, Dr. Roehl wrote several stories in the medical journal about the creation of the medical screening programs and explaining the free service offered by the community doctors.

While I was with the Mental Health Center I also worked with Indian alcoholics. I'd go to the towns of Chadron, Crawford, Gordon, Hay Springs, Rushville, Alliance, Scottsbluff, Kimball, and Sidney and stay one or two days and find out what kind of help they needed. In Gordon the Indian population was 10 percent of the total population; of that, probably 80–90 percent were alcoholics. So I got acquainted with one of the leaders in Gordon who was an Indian man by the name of Howard Scott. Howard had had some training in alcoholism. He attended AA meetings, and he knew how they operated. I told Howard that I didn't have the time to go and talk to all of the Indian people who have alcohol problems, so if he would get them together, we could have an Indian AA meeting.

We had our first AA meeting probably in the summer of 1970. I would drive from Alliance to Gordon, which is approximately seventy-five miles, and would chair the meeting. The first night it really surprised me how many people showed up. There were at least twenty to twenty-five women and men. I brought a lot of Alcoholics Anonymous literature with me. We started to hold meetings in Gordon that entire year. It was such a long distance for me to drive that I finally turned the meetings over to Howard Scott. Howard just needed a little support, and he had this now. I told him that I would create the AA programs in the rest of the towns. These programs were continued for at least five to seven years and they are still going on.

I did the same thing with the help of the Indian people in Rushville, Chadron, Crawford, and Alliance. In Alliance we held our meetings at our American Indian Center. When we first started, we had about twenty to twenty-five Indian alcoholics, mostly men with maybe a couple of women. I'd see many who were intoxicated, and I knew many had had a drink just before they came in to the meeting. I wanted to make them just as comfortable as possible, so before we started the meeting, I had Emma make a lot of sandwiches, probably enough for fifty people, and a lot of coffee. It was just something for these guys to eat. I knew that many of these men and women lived in the street, in the parks, and some of them slept in abandoned cars. They didn't have anywhere to eat or sleep.

I told them, "I just want you to come to these meetings so you can learn something about what is wrong with alcoholism." I said, "I don't care whether you're drinking now or whether you have been drinking or anything like that; I just want you to attend the meeting and learn something." So I think right away they felt quite good. When I was drinking, I was afraid to go to a place like that, but if I had the kind of support that I was trying to give these men, I probably would have sobered up. A lot of these people came to the meeting with the idea, look, I'm hungry, maybe there's somebody down there I can bum enough money off of to get a drink. I knew they came for that purpose.

But I also knew that others were honest and sincere about learning something about alcoholism. Acting as the chairman of the meeting, I told them about how I had sobered up, how much I suffered, and how hard a time I had doing it. These guys right away started talking themselves. It's usually hard to get an Indian person to speak at a meeting, but a lot of the men and women stood up and started talking. Some of these people came to the meetings intoxicated, and maybe that helped them talk about their problems. What happened in Alliance and Gordon in the AA meetings was that we were all Indian and poor, so we could all identify with each other's problems. We could identify with each other's education and living habits. There was a lot of discussion in these meetings.

Even my father, who at that time was about seventy-two or seventy-three years old and drank a lot, liked to attend these AA meetings. One night I was watching him. He went outside. There was a bush in the corner of our building where he had a pint of wine hidden, and he'd take a drink and walk back inside to the meeting. I kind of watched some of the other guys, too, and they all had something hid outside and were drinking as well. However, I couldn't bring myself to say, "Look you guys, quit your drinking or don't attend the meeting." I just couldn't do that. The only thing I was concerned about was that these guys were learning something about their problem. They were talking for once in their lives about each other's problems. It didn't make any difference to me whether they were drinking, and I didn't care whether they came down just to eat.

After the meeting was over, everybody seemed to have enjoyed it. It lasted maybe two and a half hours. After everybody started talking and feeling comfortable, I gave each one of them some literature. I don't know if the literature did any good or not, but each one of them took some and said they were going to read it. Then they had our lunch. When my wife and oldest daughter, Connie, brought the food out, these guys, who were half starved, ate up everything we had and drank up all the coffee.

I think we started something that should have been continued over these years up until right now. If finances had been available at that time, and if we had created an Indian alcoholic halfway house with an Indian alcohol program, I think we would have many more sober Indians today, and

maybe not as many people would have died. It was very sur-
prising to me how much interest in the Indian alcoholic we
drew. But I'm sure that if alcohol programs were devised to
serve Indian alcoholics, and if we had had some literature in
very simple words these people could understand, it would
have helped. I would take pictures of Indian alcoholics, how
they slept, how they ate, where they lived, and I would have
shown these pictures to them so that they could identify with
it. A lot of AA literature and even movies for educating people about alcoholism are for college-educated or high school–
educated people.

The Indian alcoholic's life in Alliance was that of a
poor Indian, with no money, with no place to sleep but an
abandoned car, and with no wife. The Indian alcoholic does
not have anything, and he drinks rotgut wine. Even if he
wanted to sober up, he wouldn't even have the support of his
community. My feeling is that conditions of class make a lot
of difference. For literature on alcoholism to be effective in
the Indian community, everything would have to be printed
in maybe third- or fourth-grade-level words, which our people could read and understand.

What was happening, I think, is that the Indian became
interested back in the 1970s, when we didn't have any way
to follow up and to support him. We just got his interest,
then dropped him. In 1972 I lost my job at the Mental
Health Center, and I could not continue these programs. I
tried at the Indian center and maybe did a lot of it, but I
didn't do as much as I wanted to. So today we still need an
Indian alcohol program for Indian people. Our alcoholism
per capita in Alliance is probably larger than any town or
any city in the state of Nebraska. The problem is getting
worse, but right now there doesn't seem to be any interest
anywhere in the Indian alcoholic.

We have here a place called Human Services where an
Indian alcoholic can go for counseling, maybe even be sent to
a detoxification center, but it doesn't work, because the In-

dian does not understand what they're trying to teach. So it's just a failure. Now, as the director of the American Indian Council, Inc., I attend a lot of meetings, church meetings, commission meetings, city council meetings, and many times I've talked to people who are in high office about trying to develop this type of program. The interest might be there, but there is no money to do anything about it, so alcohol treatment for the Indian is progressively getting worse. Some of our ten-, eleven-, twelve-year-old children are still getting drunk.

Whenever one of our staff people from the Mental Health Center would come, well, the Indian people wouldn't talk as much as they would if he wasn't there. I tried everything. I think the people on the staff knew that a program for Indian people should be devised, but nothing ever happened. They knew how to solve the problem, but they never could— but I did. I worked with many, many Indian alcoholics; part of my job was if someone in one of these areas was having DTs or getting very ill from drinking, I would drive to this area and bring that person to the Mental Health Center in Scottsbluff. The Mental Health Center would put them in the hospital (the West Nebraska General Hospital), and they would detoxify them. I never did find out who paid the bill.

I did a lot of work with alcoholics. I would arrive home at eleven or twelve o'clock at night. Maybe six or seven o'clock in the morning I'd leave again, because I was establishing so much work for myself in the whole northwestern Nebraska area, that I was on call all the time. If an Indian alcoholic in Sidney was having a problem, he was recommended to the Mental Health Center. I'd drive there, make my own recommendation, and 99 percent of the time I would drive him to Scottsbluff for counseling or for hospitalization. During this time I did have a lot of fun. It was the kind of work I liked—working with people. I wanted to help, and a lot of amusing things happened.

I remember one situation that maybe wouldn't be so

amusing to other people, but to me it was. One day, I got a call from a white lady in Gordon, Nebraska, who helped in the Gordon area, and she knew all the Indian people. Whenever an Indian had a problem, they'd call her and ask her for help. Then she would call me. One night, about eleven o'clock in the evening, this lady called me and asked me to come to Gordon and pick up this eighteen- or nineteen-year-old man and take him to the Mental Health Center. She had already called Dr. Roehl. So I told her I'd be down the first thing in the morning.

That morning I left Alliance probably six-thirty or seven and drove to Gordon. It took me the whole day to locate him. I walked down all the alleys and streets, to his friends' houses, to finally find him. I was going to have a hard time because he was still drinking, and I think he was retarded as well.

After I finally picked him up, this white lady in Gordon said, "Now don't let him out of your sight, because if you do, he is going to get drunk." I told her, "I have no way to restrain this man. He's going voluntarily and whatever he wants to do, I'll just have to go along with him." So she said to just get him up there.

I returned with this young man to Alliance, probably seven o'clock in the evening. When we got to Alliance, I called Dr. Roehl. This kid was asking for a drink, so I told Dr. Roehl and asked if I could bring him to the Mental Health Center right away. I wanted him hospitalized or detained at the Mental Health Center some way, because I knew that he wanted to go to town to get drunk. Dr. Roehl said, "No, bring him in the morning." He said I wouldn't be responsible for him getting drunk and should just let him do what he wants to do.

So the man went uptown. I had told him to come back to the center and I'd get a cot for him to sleep on, but he didn't show up. The next morning I went up town, and, sure enough, he was standing on the corner. He was so drunk and dirty, with his clothes filthy and his hair uncombed—just an awful looking sight. I told him that we had an appointment in Scottsbluff, but he wouldn't go.

I had had this problem before with many of the winos and alcoholics that I had worked with, but I found out that if you buy them another bottle, they'll do anything you want. They'll ride with you in a car, they'll work for you, whatever. I knew this wasn't the right way to do things, but I knew this man needed help. He needed another drink right away. From experience, I knew that if a man is going into delirium tremens or is very ill, another drink will pull him out of it. At this point, this young man was very ill. I told him I would give him a pint and take him up to Scottsbluff, so he said he'd go.

He got in the back of my car and I buckled him in with the seat belt. He was so wobbly and weak, I stopped at a liquor joint and bought him a pint of wine. He was so happy when he got it that he just calmed down. When we got about ten miles out of Scottsbluff to a little town by the name of Minatare, the wine wasn't enough for him. He needed another pint, but there was no liquor store to buy it. So he started getting sicker, and he didn't know how to take his seat belt off. As we were arriving at the Mental Health Center, he started throwing up in the back seat of my car.

When I drove up to the Mental Health Center parking lot, I didn't know it was ladies' day. Ladies from the fine clubs in Scottsbluff were visiting the Mental Health Center, and Dr. Roehl was giving them a tour of the building and its grounds. I kind of excused myself for what happened later on because I was just following orders. When I drove up, Dr. Roehl was with about five or six ladies, and they all were dressed up in real fine dresses and suits.

Dr. Roehl immediately came over to the car and brought these ladies with him, telling them that I was the field indigenous health care worker who brings Indian people who need mental health services to the center. Of course he did not know what had been happening in the back seat. When Dr. Roehl got to the car, he said he'd handle the patient. When he opened the door, looked inside, and saw this man, I thought he was going to change his mind, but the ladies were all circled around him and were watching. He could not stop at this point.

When he unbuckled the seat belt, the young man grabbed hold of Dr. Roehl around the neck and just rubbed against him. He was just so drunk and so sick he probably didn't even know that a white man was trying to take him into the Mental Health Center. Dr. Roehl was trying to make it look like a routine situation and like he didn't notice that his suit, necktie, face, and hair were just a mess.

Dr. Roehl put his arm around the young man and took him into the center. He warmed up some soup for him, set him down, and started feeding this soup to him. Dr. Roehl looked worse than the young man did. To this day, I don't think Dr. Roehl would have even been outside the building if he hadn't been showing those women around, but when he found himself in a real unusual spot, he had to continue what he started. I always admired Dr. Roehl for that. The ladies just kept following him, as they were very interested; a lot of them were congratulating him and telling him how good a person he was. But somehow, I suspected that underneath, Dr. Roehl was cussing the hell out of me! I'm kind of glad that the ladies stayed there all day, because I expected Dr. Roehl to chew me out.

Two or three hours later, once we put this young man in the hospital, I jumped into my car, went down to the car wash, had my car washed inside and out, and left for Alliance. When I was driving away from the Mental Health Center, I started laughing and couldn't stop for a long time. I also knew that Dr. Roehl went to a lot of trouble to get help for this young man and did a good job for him; the young man finally spent ten to twelve years in a mental health hospital.

C·H·A·P·T·E·R X

COMMUNITY ORGANIZER
Programs for Indians

There was a lot of interest in what the Panhandle Mental Health Clinic was doing, and I was being asked to talk to a number of church and other community groups in the region. I'd talk about working with alcoholics and some of the self-determination programs that I'd been able to start for Indian people. The Panhandle Mental Health Center received funds from the counties in western Nebraska. The county commissioners in each county would hear of the work I was doing, and word would filter down through the churches, and that's how I got many of my invitations to speak. I spoke at quite a few churches in 1970 and 1971, and it was good experience for my work with the American Indian Council in Alliance later. It made it much easier for me to speak to community groups about Indian problems and to raise funds for our work. I think that many of the things that I did while working at the Mental Health Center prepared me for the type of work I'm doing now. I've had a lot of experience speaking and explaining working with low-income minority people.

I also sat in on many group sessions at the center. I became real popular with the senior citizens group there, and after a while they requested that I drive to Scottsbluff each Friday afternoon for their session; after about a year, they wanted me to chair the meetings. For a couple of summers, whenever they had outings, I'd take them swimming or on a hike. These things that we did with the senior citizens practically amounted to a full-time job.

On Wednesdays and Fridays I was going to Scottsbluff, and I think sometimes I neglected my work in the Panhandle such as creating Alcoholics Anonymous programs, which were getting a lot of attention at that time. Now I was being asked to initiate Indian aid programs and to speak at the regular Alcoholics Anonymous programs, to tell them why Indian people wouldn't come to their group. I was also still working with the medical screening program, which was operating very well in Alliance, Chadron, Crawford, and all the other little towns on highway 20. During the time that I worked for the Mental Health Center, I created a lot of awareness of American Indian people in western Nebraska, but I was asked to do so many things, I just didn't have time to do them all. However, I really enjoyed working at the center; I spent probably twelve hours a day actually working, not counting all the driving from one town to another.

Another successful program started in Alliance when many of the younger people contacted me about setting up a Boy Scout troop. Indian people in Alliance were very interested in Scouts because Scouts do everything the Indian way. We held our first meeting at the American Indian Council in the first part of 1970, with fourteen boys. (As the troop progressed, many of the white boys in town saw what we were doing and asked if they could join our troop. We never restricted the group, but we started out as an all-Indian Boy Scout troop.)

In our first troop meeting I asked the boys what they wanted to do, and every one of them had his own ideas. Some of them wanted to start a Boy Scout dancing troop, and they wanted to learn how to dance and sing. I found out that none of these kids knew how to speak Indian, even though some were full-blooded Sioux. Their mothers and fathers had forgotten much about the Indian culture, especially the dancing, the language, and ceremonies. They were just like white people even though they were still Indian. I asked each boy to stand up, talk, and tell what he wanted to do. American Indian people are bashful; they don't speak out unless somebody really gets behind and pushes and supports them. So some of them had a heck of a time doing it because they were not used to speaking in groups. But I always encouraged the boys to determine their own activities, and it worked out pretty well.

I went to our Scout headquarters in Scottsbluff and got our charter. Every Scout troop has to have a parents committee to oversee them, so I formed a committee of Indian parents. We elected a chairman, vice-chairman, and Scout representatives. The parents also hated to speak up, but everybody came to the meeting; even though I had to do 99 percent of the talking, we got it going.

One of the first things I did was to contact many of the churches in Alliance that were promoting Boy Scouts and ask if they had any old uniforms and equipment for us. The churches and other organizations gave us old Scout clothes and equipment. At the meetings I fit the boys in the uniforms and their mothers sewed and cleaned them up. Some of the boys' parents had money to buy their kids their own outfits. When the boys came dressed in their uniforms, they looked real good, and they were very proud. My own two boys, Terry and Daryl, were in the troop, and I understood the pride they felt. Being a scoutmaster took up a lot of my time, but I enjoyed it a lot because it was part of community mental health services and the people's self-determination.

At our first official Scout meeting, the boys didn't seem to have much discipline as a group, so I told them, if we were going to have a Scout troop, we needed regimentation and respect for the leaders. I was going to teach them the way I had learned in the Army. I think the American Indian really respects the United States fighting forces, and some of the boys said right away they would like to learn the Scouting salute and the marching package.

So I started training them to fall in as a group and placed them in ranks. I took the taller boys, put them to the front, and the shorter boys to the back. There were sixteen of them altogether, and they all dressed in uniforms. I didn't know whether this was the Boy Scout way or not that I was teaching them, but it was the only thing I knew how to do, because this was my first time in Scouts, too. I taught them how to salute, how to march, how to turn, and other marching tactics. We had a heck of a time doing this! For about a month, we practiced inside of the large building that we have. I knew the boys would tell their parents what we were doing, and a lot of nights some of the parents were peeking in the windows.

After about a month or so, the boys would fall into their ranks perfectly and at attention; they wouldn't say anything until I gave them the command "at ease." Then they would stand in place. They were really good at this. The parents peeking in the windows were surprised at how much their kids were accomplishing, but nobody ever said anything.

Pretty soon, after the boys got to feeling comfortable in their uniforms and marching tactics, we'd go out in the park adjacent to our center. I'd walk out there, I'd tell them to fall in, and all the boys would fall directly into ranks. Gee, they looked good. We practiced out in the park, and it got to where these boys would march just like a group of soldiers. The boys really liked this because their parents would come and stand on the side of the park and watch us.

They always respected me, and I taught them how to respect their squad leaders. We had two squads of boys, and I had placed the larger boys in charge of each squad. So they were doing a lot of yes *sir*-ing and no *sir*-ing, just really paying attention. Terry, my oldest son, was elected to command this troop of Boy Scouts when they were drilling and doing their tactics. All I'd do was just stand alongside, watch, and support them. I was always awed at the way they grasped the military way of doing things. Their parents were very proud. We used to have our meetings on Monday evenings, and the parents would drive to our center to watch the boys. The boys even decided to meet Thursday or Friday nights, too, so they could get more practice. As we went along, Terry was the troop leader, and there were two boys under him who each commanded about six or seven boys in a squad. At this point, the boys were doing all of this themselves. Later on, we were invited to many parades in many towns, and I think this marching and regimentation really affected the boys in a good way.

At one meeting the troop decided that they wanted to learn how to Indian dance. Although I had danced Indian a lot in the past, I hadn't done it for so long that I had forgotten how to sing and beat the drum. But I knew that they wanted to so badly that I thought I'd better do something about it. So I contacted John White Crane, who is a very good singer and drummer, and asked him whether he would come to our meetings to teach our boys how to Omaha dance (that is what Indians call the grass dance— Omahawaci), and if he would teach them how to beat the drum and sing. When I asked John this, he was kind of afraid himself, because he had never done this before. However, I told him it would be a lot of fun working with these boys— and some of them were his nephews and grandsons. He said he'd do it.

There were a lot of things to do before we could have the first meeting with John, such as getting a drum and drum sticks. No place in Alliance had Indian drums or drum sticks, so I drove to the trading post near Wounded Knee, South Dakota, and found what we needed. A drum and six drum sticks cost about seventy-five dollars, a lot of money at that time. It would take a lot of work just preparing to get the boys dancing and singing and doing what they wanted to. I knew they needed this type of support, and so did the whole Indian community in Alliance. But I also knew that our Indian community didn't have that kind of money, and I didn't want to ask the Mental Health Center for it, so I paid for them out of my own pocket.

That first night for Indian dancing I think all the Indian people in our community knew what we were going to do. They were standing around, peeking in, kind of giggling and laughing. John was really hesitant. At this point the Boy Scouts were a little more outspoken and able to communicate with each other; they were better off than John was. The curtains didn't completely cover the windows, so we covered them with some blankets that Emma had cut up. The troop, John, and I went all around the building to see if anybody could still peek in. That night John taught each boy the dance steps, and he would sing a little bit and drum a little as he did. The boys were scared and laughing at each other, but I told them, "Look, you guys wanted to dance; now here's John to teach you. Do it."

The boys all participated, and John got a little courage and enjoyment out of it. The boys wanted to do it the next night, so we did. I think for about two weeks straight on Sunday nights and Saturday nights, these boys and John would come down. By this time, John was singing loud and clear and beating the drums. Out of the sixteen boys that were dancing, John picked about eight, and Terry was one of them. He said to me in private that the rest of the boys weren't paying enough attention, and he didn't think they had the ability to dance, but he said he'd like to teach them something. I think the eight that didn't get picked were just as happy as the ones that were. What John did was to take four of the boys who didn't get picked and let them hold the drum, and he taught them how to beat it in time with him. So everybody got to do something, and they weren't just left out.

These boys really amazed me again. They took up this Indian dancing, and they were getting good at it. John would take the boys out in the park again and let them dance there. Their parents would come down and watch them. It sounded and looked very professional to me, and I was wondering why somebody hadn't done this a long time ago. A lot of times the white people would drive by the park and would stop to watch the boys dance. The boys would draw a large crowd of people and got used to performing.

John got to the point where he liked to attend our meetings, and he just became a member of our Boy Scout committee. At one meeting John said the boys were dancing and drumming so well that we should make costumes, and he told them what to get to make their feathered dancing outfits. This created another job for me. Once again, I drove to Pine Ridge Reservation at White Clay, Nebraska, to get bells and Indian ornaments. The boys paid for the materials for their costumes themselves. John brought his own Indian dancing costume to show the boys. They did one piece at a time and would bring the piece they had finished to the next meeting until the costumes were done. I was so proud that these boys were so well disciplined, interested in their own culture and their dancing, and able to make their own costumes. This was good.

Other Scout troops in Alliance started to hear about us, and the leaders would come down to watch our boys. They were amazed, too, at how respectful and progressive these Indian boys were and how much initiative they had. We were invited to camp outings, and to the Scout Camporee at Crawford, Nebraska, with forty or fifty other Scout troops. Emma and I went up there with them and we pitched our own tent.

The boys participated in just about everything you can imagine at that three-day Camporee. Even at making pancakes, our boys excelled. By the time we left, to my amazement, they had won in every event. We had the fastest boys; they won the mile run, a quarter-mile run, and hundred-yard dash. They even won the pancake cooking contest, which the white troops had done for the past fifty years. Their performance at the Camporee at Crawford commanded a lot of respect for my boys.

When we came back to Alliance, I reported to Al Roehl on what the Boy Scout troop was doing, and he was amazed, too. This was the first time that an American Indian young man had a chance to be in these kinds of activities, and the boys just completely excelled. All the parents were happy. It kind of gave them a different attitude.

We were also invited to the Scout Camporee at the Chadron Job Corps Center with about fifty troops within the panhandle, and they had Scout Olympics. One young man, Eugene Poor Bear, was very small for his age, but he was one of the fastest kids I ever saw in my life. I entered him into a mile run at Chadron during the Scout Olympics. Eugene ran against boys who were twice his size, about thirty of them, and he so far outdistanced them that there was no competition at all. Later the papers told how well this Indian Boy Scout troop had done at the Olympics and at the Camporee. Once again, my boys won everything, and we still have our troop plaques. So the Scout troop became real well known in the western part of Nebraska.

When we came back to Alliance, our chamber of commerce director came to our center to ask if our troop would accompany him and some of his goodwill ambassadors to go to other towns, where they were promoting the Alliance Cattle Rodeo. They wanted our troop to dance in the streets in each town while the director announced the Alliance rodeo and asked people to attend. The boys were really excited about it. The chamber of commerce director had them working off the back end of a large truck. They'd drive right down the middle of the main street and park somewhere. The goodwill people would be dressed up as cowboys and be talking to everybody. Once, when it came time for our boys to dance, I think three-fourths of the town of Crawford came to see them. They were supposed to dance about four times, but the people of Crawford kept asking for more until the boys were becoming so very tired I had to stop them.

These white people probably had seen Indian dances before, but the boys danced so perfectly that they continued drawing people. I had never seen so much happiness on the boys' faces. When they got through, the people started throwing money into the street, which we never expected, dollar bills, five-dollar bills, and even ten-dollar bills. The chamber of commerce director picked up the money, $350–$400, and announced that this money was going to troop 274, the Indian Scout troop from Alliance. This really amazed the boys.

We put it into our troop fund, and used it for our equipment, new tents, and whatever we needed. That summer we started at Crawford, then worked our way east on Highway 20, dancing at Chadron, Hay Springs, Rushville, Gordon, and later at other towns; each time basically the same thing would happen. The boys got a lot of experience meeting and performing in public, and it seemed to me the more they did this, the more they enjoyed it.

We also went to the headquarters of the Panhandle Mental Health Center. The day that we performed there, the center closed up in the afternoon, and they brought the patients who were attending group therapy sessions and the staff down the street to watch our Boy Scout troop perform. To me this showed real respect on the part of Dr. Roehl and his staff at the mental health center. When Al saw the boys that I had been working with and how well they adapted to performing in public, he couldn't say enough about how pleased he was.

At the next staff meeting he started talking about how the success of the troop was an example of mental health work at its best. This was high praise from a group of people led by Dr. Roehl. I was so happy that I'd been able to organize, create, and help support this type of community activity.

That summer we also danced at the Alliance rodeo, with about six thousand people in attendance. I think when the boys performed in front of this crowd, it was probably the ultimate goal for them. When the chamber of commerce director announced that Troop 274, the Indian Boy Scout troop, would perform dancing, the crowd got on its feet and just gave them a large ovation. I think this was one of the finest things that ever happened to any minority group, and it kind of overwhelmed the boys that they were able to do something like this. They danced, and they were beautiful.

The rodeo went on for three days, and the boys performed each day and night. They became so popular here in town that afterward they were invited to private clubs to perform. I was really proud of these boys. I understand later on that many staff members of the mental health center were at the Alliance rodeo, and they couldn't say enough good words about our troop.

We were invited to Laramie Peaks where the national Scout troops meet once a year. For one week we participated in all the Scouting exercises and camped on kind of a large mountain, which the boys really enjoyed. At night they would perform for probably seven to eight thousand boys, and every time they would dance, the head scoutmaster there would introduce them as the Indian Boy Scout troop dancers. Any one of the other Scout troops who wanted to learn Indian dancing could ask, and our boys would teach them. We had a lot of fun at Laramie Peaks. It was one of the finest experiences I had in my whole life and in the lives of all the boys who attended.

Our fastest runner, Eugene Poor Bear, was picked as the official runner at Laramie Peaks to deliver messages. They didn't have any radios or telephones, it was a very remote place that we went to. Eugene delivered messages from one troop to another, and this young man would run for miles at top speed. Once again, my Boy Scout troop excelled, and they were given a lot of credit by the national Boy Scout magazine.

I can't say enough about these fine memories I have of these young men. Finally, in 1974 we disbanded our troop. The boys were getting too old to be Scouts and we could not get any younger ones to join. I think at that time there must have been some kind of generation gap. When my boys got old enough, about four or five of them joined the Army, the Navy, and the Marines. Later, these boys came to me on their furloughs and even after they got discharged. They told me how much they had received from the Boy Scout troop,

how much they had learned, and how much they had been
helped in their lives. To this day, Floyd War Bonnet, who
was a member of our troop, still comes to our center. Floyd
was in the Army, got hurt, and was never able to fully recover. He does draw a pension from the Army, and once in a
while, Floyd will come here and we will reminisce about our
troop. My oldest boy, Terry, became such a fine dancer that,
later on in his adult life, he would enter Indian dancing con-
tests and win. He won a contest here in Alliance. People
would come from Pine Ridge, Allen, South Dakota, all our
Indian neighbors to the west, and Terry would win these con-
tests. He was very proud of his ability, and I was, too. It sure
makes me feel good because I think at that time we were able
to create something new in Alliance for our young people.

Another community program was requested by the
adults during our Indian Center meetings. Some of the people
had always wanted a garden but didn't have enough room to
start one near their homes. The center building was adjacent
to four or five blocks of empty lots. I talked to the city council and got permission to utilize these lots to plant gardens.
Probably twenty to twenty-five Indian families participated;
they would come down and spade their own site, plant, and
take care of this garden. What I saw was that the people
were doing something they always wanted to do. Given a
chance, they did a good job. The people spent all of their off-
work hours working there. The mayor of our town congratulated us in the news media about the large garden we had in
South Alliance being tended by Indian people and how nice
the garden looked and how well it was taken care of. I never
saw more happy people than during the harvesting of this
garden. I think the garden and the participation of Alliance
Indian residents really was a change. You could see it in the
attitude of the people and their pride.

One of the most important things that we did was to
create a program for tutoring Indian children who were slow
in school. One of the problems brought out at our meetings

was that many of our Indian children were behind white children and didn't understand the subjects they were taking in
school. So what I did was to contact teachers in Alliance who
would come to our Indian center and tutor these children
who needed it. We probably had fifteen teachers who would
volunteer every night, Monday through Friday, during the
school year. It really helped out Indian children in their
school work, and I really enjoyed sitting in on the tutoring
sessions and learned a lot from it, too. We also began a GED
testing program for Indian adults.

After running for police magistrate and working for the
Mental Health Center, I had created so much awareness of
the Indian community that I was invited by the Northwest
Nebraska Community Action Program (CAP) to sit on a
board of directors of the Emergency Food and Medical Service, which was created by the federal government to serve
low-income people. My wife had put in an application for a
job with the service, but I was on the board of directors and
told the director of the Northwest CAP that my wife had applied for the job. He said that was all right as long as I didn't
vote on it or support her in any way. So I didn't, but Emma
had the best qualifications for it, and she received the position as a worker in the Emergency Food and Medical Service
department.

Basically, her job was at our center, as the CAP gave
her permission to work here in Alliance and to give food and
medical services for low-income people. The reason for this
was because we had already created the medical screening
program, and Emma's job was to extend this program. She
was very good at it. She had become a nutrition specialist by
attending many classes. Then she hired an assistant for herself
with the pay coming from Northwest CAP. This is one example of the way our center was very helpful to low-income
people, creating paying jobs such as Emma's.

During meetings of the Indian people and some of the
low-income white people, the discussion of Indian alcoholism

always came up. The same questions were asked at the Pan-handle Mental Health task meetings—why there were so many Indian alcoholics, why so many of them went to recovery centers but nothing worked. So many questions being asked but no answers being given. At that time in the state of Nebraska, 85 percent of all Indian people were alcoholics or came from an alcoholic family or had an alcohol problem. With all this discussion going on, there was a lot of awareness. I began to look upon myself as an Indian alcohol expert even though I didn't have any degrees from college, or from a school. Today, you need education and degrees because that's what people believe in and hire you for. However, I think my going through the experience I had gave me my ability to work with all kinds of alcoholics—Indian, white, and Mexican—I was able to work well, and to solve some of their problems.

After a lot of discussion with Dr. Roehl, I was given approval and some funds to start an alcohol program for minority people. So I began to visit other alcohol centers in the state of Nebraska. I asked Rev. Don Meek, who was pastor of our Church of God Indian Mission in Alliance and was very active and concerned about Indian alcoholism, to go with me to a mental hospital in Hastings that accepted alcoholics of all races and income brackets.

Rev. Don Meek and I drove up there, and to me it seemed like heaven because they had such a good program. Nothing like what I had gone through. People were becoming more aware of alcoholism and were creating AA programs. We were asking how to start a halfway house for recovering alcoholics and were given a lot of information. We also went to Grand Island, to another recovery center. We came back to Alliance, and I was chosen by our community meeting of Indian people and low-income white people to initiate an alcohol halfway house.

I contacted many of the ministers here in Alliance, the city officials, and county commissioners, and created a board of about eleven men, some very prominent people in our area. At our first meeting I explained to them the conditions of the Indian alcoholic and of all minority, low-income alcoholics who had the problem but could not receive any help. Everybody agreed that we needed a halfway house in Alliance. Everybody was in agreement because they were reading constantly in the paper about Indian people being picked up for intoxication and for drunk driving. I was elected chairman of the board.

We were going to call our halfway house the Panhandle Alcohol Rehabilitation Center. We wanted to receive funds from churches, from the city of Alliance, and from the county to run a house for approximately twelve people. Everything worked fine, and we got a lot of support. There were many write-ups in the paper. This alcohol detoxification center started out with eight men, and I was in complete charge of it. We didn't have any paid counselors, as I did all this work voluntarily as director. Whenever an alcoholic would want to recuperate, we would take him to the house on the recommendation of a police officer or doctor. I rented a house, had the lights and gas and everything turned on, and put the men in there. It was kind of an honor system that these guys would take care of the building themselves at night.

However, there was dissension among members of the board of directors. The alcohol halfway house was for anybody who wanted to come, but I was recommending that we work only with low-income people. Although I had spent many hours getting the board of directors together, finding the house, and getting information, I was finally voted off the board. The white people took over the operation of it. There really were no bad feelings, and I just continued my own work.

The Panhandle Alcohol Rehabilitation Center (PARC) worked well for about four years. At one time, they even rented a larger house that would accommodate about twenty alcoholics. What they wanted to do was enlarge and increase the number of people they were going to serve, but a lot of alcoholics were complaining that they weren't getting the services. After about four years a couple of people who were administering the program were charged with mismanagement of funds and the program folded. It was needed badly, so I was sorry about what happened.

I met with Dr. Roehl several times about the Panhandle Alcohol Rehabilitation Center and told him that PARC was not going to last. Al finally expressed his feelings that I was right and he was wrong. I knew that a halfway house for Indian alcoholics would have to be governed and administered by Indian people so their needs would be respected and given preference. With Indian administration, it would survive. Because I was speaking out during the board meetings of PARC, I hurt a lot of people's feelings.

It was about this time that Ken Lincoln, Al Logan Slagle, a lawyer friend of Ken's, and I drew up a proposal for a halfway house in Alliance to treat Indian alcoholics. In it, we described all of the programs we were providing such as a nutrition program, a medical screening program, an alcoholism counselor (myself), weekly busing trips of patients to the BIA (Bureau of Indian Affairs) hospital and public health services at Pine Ridge, a CETA job-training program, and much more. We also pointed to all the recreational activities offered by the American Indian Council—the Indian Boy Scout troop, community clean-up program, Indian dancing, baseball teams, bingo, and quilting. We pointed out that all these programs had operated successfully, some for fifteen years. Our idea was to send this proposal to all the local and state organizations that might be interested in providing funding.

We wanted to buy the Tekawitha Hall from the Roman Catholic church for $5,000. This was a large steel Quonset-hut type of building across the street from our center. On the unused lots overlooking Indian Creek we could build a Lakota sun shade, a community garden, and a truck farm.

(A Lakota sun shade is a place for pow-wows, dancing, and the like. It is built in a circle with pine tree stakes covered with cedar boughs to shade the spectators.) A tree nursery nearby could also provide jobs as well as a HUD housing project for low-income people.

Recovering alcoholics could live at the halfway house, with the American Indian Council serving as their home base, and the Indian community in Alliance as their extended family. This kind of relationship is important for Indian people. We felt we wanted to offer an experimental approach to the treatment of alcoholism. The inmates could either stop drinking altogether or learn to control their drinking habits. We also wanted to provide some of the Indian healing methods. Medicine men and tribal elders could serve as advisers for the use of the sweat lodge, fasting, and vision quest along with other therapies and medicines used in Indian healing.

The rules for running such a program could be drawn up by the recovering alcoholics themselves so that the halfway house would provide a supportive environment. In addition to having social opportunities and teaching good eating habits, we would be providing counseling and employment as well. Most important, the inmates would have a say in how the program was run. This was the Indian way of doing things, used by tribes in their decision making for generations.

Although I knew such a program could work, we never did get funded. Potential funders objected to our experimental approach to alcoholism and failed to appreciate that treating Indian alcoholics is very different from treating whites. To this day, a halfway house in Alliance is a pipe dream. An alcohol rehabilitation center for Indian alcoholics is still needed because conditions are worse now than they were then.

Emma continued to work for the Emergency Food and Medical Service. She was able to create a lot of programs herself, and I helped her. Emma was not used to really doing this kind of work, but she learned very fast. She started nutrition programs at the Indian center. Every week Emma and her boss would hold nutrition classes to teach low-income women how to cook the finest food at the lowest prices possible. When this was done, a large meal would be cooked and fed to the women who attended. It was very popular and lasted probably five or six years. Sewing classes were also very popular. Emma and her boss would start with a whole fashion show once a month, and the ladies who sewed their own dresses would go up on stage and show them off. These things were really working well and were all done at our American Indian Center.

One thing I was always so happy about was that my wife was also involved in what I was doing. Not only were we both involved in working for CAP, but we would hold our own meetings at the center, and she would recommend Indian people as representatives whom we elected to sit on the Community Action board of directors.

At this time I had two jobs, one for the Panhandle Mental Health Center and one as director of the American Indian Council without pay. We were very busy in Alliance; this was a fast part of our lives, but it was a good part, too. With the support of the Mental Health Center and the support of the Northwest Community Action Program, we were able to get a lot of Indian people and other low-income minority people involved in talking, expressing their concerns and their problems. State officials thought what we were doing in Alliance was really very interesting, and some of them would attend our meetings. This participation by the state officials was good for the Northwest Community Action Program because it was also funded by the federal government.

During the time I worked for the Mental Health Center, I became well known in this part of the state. I sat in with psychiatrists as they were talking with their patients, and with Al Roehl as he was talking with his. I worked with psychiatric nurses and was a leader of group therapy. I taught the staff of the Mental Health Center and the community mental health programs how to go into a low-income community and teach low-income people self-respect, how to survive, and how to solve some of their problems such as alcoholism. I was in the right place at the right time. I discovered that I had the ability to administer; I was always good at figures, and I had the ability to lead. The state director of mental health services often would come right out during a meeting and congratulate me on the type of work that I was doing. Then he'd turn around and tell the staff just the way it should be done. I think this angered many of the staff people at the Mental Health Center, as these people were highly educated. I do not have a degree in anything as I am a self-taught man, but I've actually had the problem that these people had learned about in books. That made it very easy for me to express my thoughts. But I think my doing the work in the center and in the community caused a lot of the staff members to dislike me, even though they wouldn't openly tell me so. Toward the end of my job at the Mental Health Center, Al Roehl asked me to meet privately with him. I don't know whether it was because of jealousy or whether I was creating too much tension or just doing too good of a job, but he asked me not to attend the staff meetings anymore. It kind of hurt my feelings, but I can say truthfully that I never did go out of my way to offend any of the staff people as I liked every one of them. I respected them, and I think they did me, too.

Toward the end of the three-year period that I worked there, my only true friend was Bob Bontrager, our social worker. He had a master's in social work. He was about the same kind of guy I was—joking and happy about everything. I asked him about why I was asked to stay away from the staff meetings, and he said that I had stepped on a few toes I shouldn't have. He basically thought that some people felt I was an Indian getting out of line. Then he told me that he was going to Oregon to be the director of Oregon State Mental Health Services, and he asked me to work for him there.

It was such a good offer. Bob was honest and likable, and he was a very good friend. I told him, "Bob, I don't know. I don't know the Indian people out there. They are completely different from us and speak a different language and have different customs, so I don't know whether I'd be able to work with them." But he said, "Mark, you can do it." But I was scared, so I discussed it with Emma a long time. To this day I still wonder why I turned the job down. Emma wanted to go, but I knew that she was doing real good in the community and was happy with her job. Even though I didn't like what was happening at the Mental Health Center, I was very happy that I had sobered up and that I had become a good productive citizen. I was concerned about moving my family. I was really content, you might say, with the way things were.

I had worked with the Mental Health Center from March 1969 to March 1972, and all this time I really enjoyed it. But in March of 1972 I was very kindly and quietly fired. The reason why I was fired was that in the latter part of 1971 and early part of 1972, I was beginning to have personal problems with Emma, which we could not solve or adjust to. I think it was probably February 1972 that I started drinking. I got on a good drunk. I want to mention this here because I think it was a very significant learning experience for me as an alcoholic. Even though I did drink, I drank beer. I think that makes a lot of difference, and I didn't drink as much as I had in the years before going to Fort Meade. After I got fired, I went into a deep depression and would sit around and think about all the good I had done while sober and what happened to me. I think our family problems could have been solved better than by my getting drunk, but at this time Emma began to drink, too. In other words, I felt sorry for myself. I knew that I had gone back into the same disease that I hated and that had meant spending over two years in a detoxification center. I would sit around and think about these things.

When I started to drink again, a lot of Indian friends who did not socialize with me during the time I was sober became my friends again, and I would drink and spend my money on them. (Emma and I had saved up a little money by this time.) I spent until August 1973 drinking this way. I still lived in the Indian center, working with the Boy Scout troop and with everything else that we had created. I think the Indian community knew that I was drinking, but I don't think the white community did, unless it was the people who fired me, the board of directors of the Panhandle program. I drank beer very quietly but didn't go bum on the streets and didn't fall down any alleys. But somewhere inside of me I knew that I had lost one of the greatest treasures that I ever had, and that was my sobriety. Every time I would drink, I would sit down and think about this. I wanted it back. I could tell that Emma was thinking about this, too. Even though we didn't mention it, we were both thinking that we had known a good life. I knew that I would have to completely quit drinking, get myself back on my feet, and help Emma get back on hers. I knew that if I quit drinking, she would, too. Our children were pretty well grown by this time, and they were suffering from what I had done again. I felt that I had committed the biggest sin that any person could commit. I think I had become a social drinker or maybe a weekend drinker. I kind of liked it because I'm a person who loves alcohol, but I'm also a person who cannot drink. In my times of sobriety I read books and had learned from people that an alcoholic can never drink again. Emma continued working for the Community Action Program, but I was without a job. I think this is what hurt me the most. During this period of over a year I did a lot of mental suffering and wishing I could get back to the point where I had been.

In August 1973 I went out in the front of our building

in the center and was sitting at my desk looking at our bank account when I noticed that in the past two weeks I had spent five hundred dollars on beer and buying drinks for my friends. It took me over three years to earn this money, but it took me only two weeks to drink it up. At this point I became very angry at the so-called Indian friends who enjoyed seeing me drunk again. An alcoholic Indian has no support system when he is sober because Indians would not support a sober Indian. So that day as I was sitting at my desk, it came to my mind from somewhere that I was going to quit drinking. I didn't want to go into Fort Meade for rehabilitation or to Hot Springs again. I just stopped drinking that day. Since August 1973 I have not had one drink, and I'm very, very proud of it. At this point in my life I don't even think about alcohol or crave it. That day I made a decision by myself that I didn't have to be hospitalized or institutionalized. All I needed was will power.

Sometimes even today we'll sit around, and I'll be talking with Butch or one of my close friends in Alliance, when they'll ask me how long I have been sober. And I'll say, "I've been sober since 1968," even though this happened to me in the years of 1972 and 1973. It was one of the biggest learning experiences in alcoholism that any person could ever have. I learned that an alcoholic cannot drink and that he can make up his mind to quit. He does not have to be hospitalized or institutionalized involuntarily. In that 1972–73 part of my drinking, I learned more about Indian alcoholism than I had done in the entire time I worked with Indian alcoholics. I learned that a man can make a mistake and lose one of the greatest gifts of his life. I also learned that if he wanted this gift back and wanted it back bad enough, he would do something about it.

Sometimes sitting here by myself I wonder if it was God's way of showing me the problems in alcoholism. Some people quit and quit for the rest of their lives, which is what I am doing now. Some people will go back and drink and drink until they're a gutter-type alcoholic. Shortly after I made the decision to quit—it was Thanksgiving of 1973— Emma put the turkey on the table. Something came into my mind, and I was very, very happy. What I thought about was, I'm sober, I'm not dependent upon alcohol any more. That was one of the finest Thanksgivings I ever had in my life.

I had something to be thankful for, and I'm proud of myself and proud of my wife and my children. Since that day, everything has worked well, even though I've lost some of the most beloved people in my family. That learning experience of sobering myself up may have helped and prepared me for what I had to go through later on in my life.

C·H·A·P·T·E·R XI

THE AMERICAN INDIAN COUNCIL
Speaking for Ourselves

The American Indian Council was established in February of 1973. When we got our state charter and changed the name of our organization from the American Indian Committee to the American Indian Council, Inc., I was pretty sure that we would be able to reach all our goals. With tax-exempt status, we were ready to obtain funds. Indian people were utilizing the screening program and going to see the local doctors, and some were getting their prescribed medications free. But we had no support for those who needed hospitalization. Emma suggested that if we had a large vehicle, we could take whoever needed to be hospitalized to Pine Ridge. The board directed me to go to each county that we would be working with and ask them for funds, telling them why we needed money and about the need for hospitalization for Indian people. The busing program started in December 1972 on a trial basis.

I made good progress with the busing program, contacting Box Butte County, Dawes County, and Sheridan County. Dawes and Sheridan counties are on the way to Pine Ridge from Alliance. When I had the okay from Pine Ridge Hospital about taking patients there, the road was clear for us to start receiving funds. Each county agreed to pay us $150 a month for gas, oil, and a small salary. I'm very good at keeping books and accurate accounts of receipts and expenditures, so I utilized that ability to get the busing program well on its way. We were still using the old Community Action bus to transport people, but everybody was happy. They would use the medical screening program to go to doctors here. If they needed to go to the hospital, we had that follow-up program. Everything seemed to be working good.

During this time I was still drinking at home and with my friends at their homes, mostly hidden drinking. But a lot of people knew about it. Some people, like my mother and mother-in-law, were angry with me whenever I drank, but I had done a lot for the community so they just accepted it and said, "Well, if he is going to drink, let him drink." I understood that attitude but I knew I had to do better.

After I decided in August 1973 to completely quit drinking, I was happier than when I first sobered up. I continued my community work and did some manual labor again, for the first time in many years.

By the end of the year, a man from the Alliance Jaycees came to me and told me that they had given me the good citizenship award for 1973. It was a nice plaque. The award read: "The Alliance Jaycees present a good citizenship award to Mark Monroe. Mark Monroe and his wife, Emma, have five children. Since 1969, Mark has been involved in the social and community development for Indians and low-income people in the Alliance community. Since he has been with the American Indian Center, he has started such programs as the Medical Screening Program to get medical aid for the poor, a Boy Scout troop, the Medical Busing Program to take Indians to Pine Ridge Hospital, an Alcoholics Anonymous Program and Nutritional Center for the poor, a GED test program so adults can get their high school diplomas and a cleanup project to clean lots in South Alliance. The only way to solve a problem Mark knows is to get involved in the community." I felt very guilty about getting back on drink, but I think the award was their people's way of telling me that they were glad to see me sober again.

My work was also being recognized by people outside of Alliance. The state had started the Nebraska Indian Commission; I was one of the Indian people that Governor Exon appointed to sit on the commission to serve the northwest part of the state. I was very proud of this, and the Indian people I was serving here in Alliance were very happy for me too. I was not only able to represent Alliance but also to make a lot of contacts in Lincoln and Omaha for the betterment of our programs. About the same time the governor also appointed me to the Fort Robinson Centennial Commission, which would commemorate an old Army post out here in Nebraska. I was very busy, working with state business, even before I stopped drinking; no one cared about whether I drank. What they saw was a man who was able to produce; they were looking for a leader.

Near the end of 1973 my mother-in-law, Jenny Lone Wolf, held an Indian *lowanpi,* or an Indian sing, a ceremony in which a holy man comes to treat Indian people and make them well. The Indian medicine man who came was a very good friend of mine, Joe Chips. Joe always liked to drink beer, so when he came, I had a six-pack for him, but I did not drink with him. That night the *lowanpi* took place in complete darkness, with nobody talking or anything; Mr. Chips healed a lot of people. It was either Emma or my mother-in-law who had asked Mr. Chips to help me obtain a good-paying job somewhere. The next morning Emma told me that Joe Chips had said that I would get a better job and do more for my people than ever before. He said she should tell me not to worry. When Emma told me that, it kind of brought me back to seeing how things were falling into place. Joe Chips has died since then, but everything he said did come true. I think I have led a very comfortable life, and I have been able to create my own job where I have been free to do what I wanted to do and to help the needs of the people. I'm always very thankful for his look into the future.

I met a young lady by the name of Jan Wallen in Lincoln. She was working for the Nebraska Indian Commission at that time. Later, she was hired by the United Indians of Nebraska, a statewide Indian organization. I was also elected by our Indian community in Alliance to represent them in this organization. So I was working on two different boards at one time, the Nebraska Indian Commission and the United

Indians of Nebraska. When I went to these meetings, a lot of Indian people would get drunk and stay drunk all night long. The next day, they weren't worth a darn—they couldn't talk, and they couldn't represent—but I was cold sober. This I think helped me in so many ways. It drew the respect of all the people who were representing the Santee tribe, the Winnebago tribe, the Omaha tribe, and the local people in Omaha and Lincoln. They knew that when I went to these meetings, I was a sober businessman. They respected me for it. They elected me vice-chairman of the Nebraska Indian Commission, which was the commission working directly under the governor, and that put me in a very high position—a position of making a lot of decisions affecting Indian people.

The Nebraska Indian Commission was not a funding organization; they were more of an Indian advocate. But the United Indians of Nebraska did provide some funding for programs that were good and needed to be funded. With my position as vice-chairman, I was in a very good position to bring money out into western Nebraska. And I did. When I told them about our medical busing and screening programs, they funded both programs.

In 1973 everything seemed to fall into place for us. My family was very happy. I was able to create programs where we could manage our own money and administer it. As I've said many times now to some of the church groups that I speak to, the American Indian Council is an example of the philosophy of self-determination. We are self-governed and self-administered. We use church and county money, but we're able to do the work ourselves. I am very proud that we have learned how to do this and that it is one of the proudest aspects of my life. There are white people who compete with us to perform the same services, but when I bring up the fact that we are self-governed and self-administered, people can see we are a product of the kind of self-determination that the church is asking for. Nobody ever questions us. The church's philosophy that Indians were capable of doing things for themselves was good.

As I mentioned before, our medical busing program had an old 1965 Ford van that did not have a heater, cooling system, or radio. Basically, all it had was four wheels and a van chassis. Many times when we took people to the Pine Ridge Hospital, they would be sicker when we got there than when we left. It was so cold in winter. During the summertime when it was so hot, it made them very uncomfortable. In March or April of 1974, Emma and I attended an interchurch ministry meeting in Lincoln. Our Presbyterian church here was a member of this group. When we got through with the meeting, the minister came down and said, "Mark, I've got a surprise for you." He gave me a check for $5,000 and a letter with the check saying it was for the purchase of a new van to bus people to the Pine Ridge Hospital.

I was totally astonished as I had not submitted a proposal to the Self-development of People Committee. I was amazed at how this money had come to be offered to us. It seems Rev. Osborne, the minister at the Presbyterian church, and our local church had submitted a proposal for a new van for us. When I got back to Alliance, I immediately called a meeting of the board of directors and gave them the news. They were very surprised and happy and directed me to purchase a new van. Just a day or two later I bought a 1974 Suburban GMC, which could haul eleven people.

I owe so much to the Presbyterian people that sometimes I don't know how to thank them enough. When I speak at many church functions and ladies' church groups, I never forget to tell them how caring and compassionate Presbyterians are. Again in 1984 the church's Self-development of People Committee purchased a new van for us, which we are using now. It has got probably 76,000 miles on it. I think you can understand how I feel about the Presbyterian church.

In my experience, the programs run by American Indians themselves are the successful ones. In 1974 the director of the senior citizens' organization in Alliance called me up and wanted to know how many people sixty years old and over we had, as they wanted them to come to the nutrition program. Well, at that time my parents and Emma's parents, and about six or seven other Indian people were eligible for this program. I'd bus them to the program every noon; whenever Emma and I would go, they would serve us too. We did this for about a month. The people at the senior citizen's nutrition program separated the Indian people from the whites and served them last. Sometimes there wouldn't be enough food left for our people. I didn't want to say anything for fear that I'd ruin something good for the elderly people. But after a month some of them were saying they didn't want to go to the nutrition program anymore and wouldn't tell the reason. The last time we took people over there, only two or three went, and they didn't really want to go.

At one of our community meetings we brought up the nutrition program, and three or four of the Indian senior citizens told us that they didn't want to go because they felt they didn't belong there, that they weren't treated right, and they just didn't seem to fit in. People asked me if there was any possibility of starting a nutrition program ourselves. I told them we could always look into it, but I couldn't promise anything because money was so hard to get. Then one morning, the manager of one of our local stores called me on the phone and asked me to go down to his store to see what was happening there. In back of his store, there were probably twenty to twenty-five Indian people, maybe eight or nine of them women, fighting for food like old rolls and lunch meat and canned goods that had been thrown out in the dumpster. When I saw this, it made me feel so ashamed. I knew that we had winos here in town in large numbers, but I didn't know they existed this way until I saw it for myself. (When I was drinking, I was never hungry because I couldn't eat.) I just made up my mind that I was going to get some money to start a nutrition program to feed these people and others as well. I started checking my resources to figure out who would be interested in this type of program. I also made sure that our other programs were running well because I knew that a program like this would take a lot of time and effort to get started.

I went to Rev. Osborne and told him about our senior citizens and the alcoholics fighting behind the store. He knew all about it, but hadn't been able to get enough funds to do something. He said that if I could get a program started, he'd try to get the church to contribute. Then I brought this problem up at a meeting of the Nebraska Indian Commission, and the group offered their support in our quest for funds. Then I wrote a one-page proposal asking for $600 or $700 to start the program and presented it in Omaha to the United Indians of Nebraska meeting. They funded it immediately.

I knew that if the program got publicity in the cities of Alliance, Omaha, and Lincoln, we would be able to begin. When I returned to Alliance, I told our council board of directors that we had enough money to start a program, and on September 16, 1974, we opened our nutrition program. Our policy at that time was and still is to feed anyone who declares hunger, regardless of age, race, or sex. This might be the policy in soup kitchens and church kitchens in larger cities, but in a rural area like ours, ours was the first unrestricted program.

On the first day we served twenty-five alcoholics. These guys came to the meal dirty, with their hair uncombed and their clothes filthy. My mother-in-law would pray at each meal before the meal was served. She also would tell the Indian alcoholics, "Mark has done this for us. Mark has received funds to start a meal program." She told them in Indian that the next time they came they should at least clean themselves up. "At least comb your hair, wash your faces; we will give you a free meal but you give us some respect," she said. Most of the alcoholics really respected my mother-in-law, who was Nick Black Elk's cousin. They didn't say anything, but before they left, I made my little speech, too. I told them basically the same thing she did, that we were opening this program, and I hoped it lasted for many, many years, but all we were trying to do was keep them alive and give them something to eat. In return, I wanted them to respect us, too, to respect my staff, my mother-in-law, and the elderly people who eat here. That's all we asked.

The next day, I was going to town to shop for the cooks. I drove by South Park, which some people called Indian Park; it's the place where most Indian alcoholics stay and sleep. I looked out there and saw probably around fifteen to twenty men and women standing in a group around the little creek that runs through the park. I slowed down because I wondered what they were doing. I thought maybe someone had drowned or something terrible had happened. But as I looked over, I saw that the alcoholics were standing there washing their faces, combing their hair, and getting themselves cleaned up. I thought that what my mother-in-law had said and what I had said really must have affected them. When I was drinking, I didn't listen to anybody. All I wanted to do was drink.

When I came home, I didn't say anything to the staff—Emma, who was the cook, and her sister, Dorothy, who was her assistant. We were ready to serve about eleven-thirty. The girls peeked out of the door and saw everybody standing out there with faces washed up and their hair combed. Dorothy ran right back into the kitchen and told Emma to come and take a look at these people. They sure looked good, all cleaned up and lined up for us to open the door. The respect that these alcoholics showed us was something new. I don't think they had ever done that before.

We started getting private and church donations; Rev. Osborne was very effective in getting funds for our programs. We were the only organization in the state of Nebraska who had this type of program, and everybody in Alliance was proud of it. Our year-end reports show that from its beginning in 1974 to the end of 1993, the program served 106,931 meals to 2,987 different people: 1,079 Indians, 1,079 whites, 443 Mexican-Americans, and 49 blacks.

Right now we're having some funding problems, but we have tried to prove to Alliance and the nation that hunger exists here and that the nutrition program is one of the most needed programs that we have. There were times we had to close the program for at least half the year because of lack of funds. I have attended every meeting where a proposal for our nutrition program was presented, and I think the local people and those who are sitting on national boards have a hard time accepting the fact that hunger exists in the United States. They don't want to believe it. Every town in western Nebraska that has a large Indian community has a hunger problem, but it also affects whites, Mexican-Americans, and blacks. Once hunger is recognized as a problem, it will be much easier for us to get funding for our program. I think there is more hunger now than when we first began the program in 1974. Every day I see more people going through town on the train who are bumming. I talk to many of these people, and many of them are well-educated people who have lost their jobs and are here looking for employment.

Our busing program, which is a very good program, is still in effect. We are busing more people than ever. In 1993 we bussed 648 people, which would be an average of about eleven or twelve people per trip. Our bus is a twelve-passenger van. Every week on Tuesday since the beginning of the program on December 19, 1972, to December 31, 1993, 10,847 people were transported to the Pine Ridge Hospital in South Dakota. In addition, 105 people were transported on an emergency basis—that is, on other days of the week, when a person was too sick to wait until the next Tuesday. I've shown the county commissioners that our medical busing program saves each county we serve approximately $45,000 to $48,000 a year in indigent medical care. If these people were hospitalized in their respective communities and not in Pine Ridge Hospital, the county would have to stand the cost of hospitalization.

The people have asked for these programs themselves. They have seen their own need and requested someone who

could administer and develop them. Having community meetings and getting the solution to the problem developed
through these meetings has worked effectively and is getting
the job done. To this day we are still offering them. We have
to operate on the larger scale because conditions at present
for low-income people and even the middle class are getting
worse. The unemployment rate is very high, creating more
low-income citizens, and there is less funding available to
handle the great need.

As I discussed earlier, many of our Indian people were
not well educated and were unemployed or had irregular
jobs. We were giving GED classes at our Indian center so that
Indians could get their high school diplomas, but we needed a
program to get people jobs. In 1975 I attended a Nebraska
Indian Commission meeting on the Santee Reservation where
a white man asked me if we had the Indian Manpower Program in western Nebraska. I told him I had never heard of it.
So he suggested that we start training Indian people on the
CETA program. Within a month's time he came to a western
Nebraska community meeting, told us how to organize, how
to set up a board of directors for handling federal money,
and how to run and administer the program. He said that as
soon we had the structure, we could get people trained for
jobs paying a minimum wage. That very night the people
elected me as the administrator to start and operate the
CETA program from our Indian center.

When this man from Santee saw all this happening, he
went back and immediately sent us funds to start the new
program. I, in turn, started going to Gordon, Scottsbluff,
Chadron, and here in Alliance, creating an advisory board. I
was not involved in the hiring process, but I told each city to
elect two representatives to the board of directors. These representatives would then do the hiring in their own community.

After I started receiving funds, getting it into the bank,
and getting the checkbooks made, I could have used a secre-

tary, but I decided I'd rather use the funds to hire another person for the training part of it. So, I was administrator as well as secretary. We began June 1975, and I immediately put at least twelve Indian people to work in good training positions. Everything worked well for us. I'd always wanted to work with federal and state money, and now I had finally accomplished that.

When I started administering the CETA program in Alliance, Jan Wallen, who was then with the United Indians of Nebraska, also sent a proposal to the CETA Indian Manpower Program. In the latter part of 1975 she, as the director, was given a program to administer. That made things much easier for me. When United Indians of Nebraska received the program, I was not only on their board, but also the administrator of the CETA program in western Nebraska. They said that I could not be both, but Jan told them I was the only Indian person in the area who had the qualifications and the ability to run the program. When some of the board members from Omaha came out to Alliance to investigate the problem, they saw that we had a center and active programs going. They made some changes in their bylaws that allowed me to hold both offices, and it worked out well.

The CETA program lasted from 1975 to the latter part of 1981. In this time I was able to train 157 Indian people, and the statistics that I sent to Jan Wallen and the United Indians of Nebraska proved that 57 percent of the people had been placed in permanent jobs. It became such a big undertaking that I had to hire an administrative assistant who could travel to the Panhandle, where the closest towns are sixty to seventy miles apart. I think we did a real good job of it, but the CETA program ended in 1981. I understand that CETA is still operating but under a different title. The only thing that they do now is offer GED classes for high school diplomas.

With the state of Nebraska, we developed a program that hired Indian medical aides. It was completely separate from the Indian programs we had started as it was a white program but administered by Indian people. That program worked well, and I think Jan Wallen followed up on it and brought in the Indian Health Service Program from the U.S. government, which was the same thing as the medical aide program we had through the state. Up until 1982 the Indian Health Service Program medical aides were still working in this area. They were administered by the American Indian Council. The medical aide would go into Indian or low-income white people's homes and see whoever had called for assistance. They were paraprofessionals who would refer patients to the doctors or sometimes do the medical work themselves.

The Indian people really benefited from these programs. Many got permanent jobs, and others got training for work. What I wanted to do first of all was teach the American Indian to go to work at seven in the morning and get off at five, or whatever the job required. I wasn't too interested in what the man or woman learned. My primary involvement would be to teach people how to go to work, because many of our Indian people had never been employed before. Many did not have any education. They weren't ready for regimentation, and they could not stand it. This was one of the things that was wrong with me in my earliest years. Then the second thing I wanted to do was to place one or two in our Indian Center in our nutrition program and some in daycare centers and some in the school system. I would make sure they'd go and work the entire day. The employer told me that many of the Indian people who were trained in our program came to work on time, and that they worked till their required time was up.

Our only problem was with the American Indian Movement (AIM), which was becoming active in Alliance and in northwest Nebraska. When I first heard about it, I was very proud and happy that we had a national organization that believed in Indian unity. It made me feel we had an Indian advocate. However, AIM was against everything that we had ever done in Alliance. The fact was, although they were asking for unity, they were creating problems among Indian people.

Every time that we had a meeting, AIM was present. They were argumentative about everything we had done, and they were mostly against me because we had some strong philosophical differences. If any AIM members asked me about hiring practices, I protected myself by answering that I did not do the hiring. The representative from each area did that. I would tell them I merely put people on the payroll, kept the books, and wrote their checks. Even though there was a lot of conflict, I never really ran into a problem, but the representatives did.

AIM came into Alliance in 1972, just after Raymond Yellow Thunder was killed in Gordon, Nebraska. They came to Alliance for the trial of the men who killed Mr. Yellow Thunder, and to see that the trial was fair. So I thought that by doing that, AIM was doing its job. I think all the Indian people were infuriated because of the degrading things that had been done to this man before they killed him.

At that time the philosophy of the American Indian Council stated that we did not believe in violence, that we wanted to work within the system that we have to live in, that we would respect all laws of the cities and state, and that if we wanted to know anything, such as why we were mistreated, we would ask. We never violated any laws. I have always believed that this is the way to act to get your rights explained to you. If we needed anything, I'd go directly to the source that could help us, and it usually worked out. I think it is a matter of understanding on both sides, the white side and the Indian side, and it seems to be working yet today.

When the national AIM leaders came to Alliance from Denver, I was the first one they contacted. The leaders came to our Indian Center, and I served them rolls and coffee. Approximately two to three hundred people came to town, and they seemed to me to be a very violent, militant group. Some of the men had guns and knives, and some were intoxicated. Many were on dope. As soon as I saw this, I didn't like it. But I was very afraid. I didn't want to say anything because I believed that Indians had the right to come because they were very mad about the Yellow Thunder trial. At that time, I still continued to support AIM, and I did everything I could for the national Indian movement. AIM stayed here, and they saw what they thought was a fair trial. However, I never did think it was fair, because the men who killed Mr. Yellow Thunder received very light sentences. After the trial the American Indian Movement stayed in Alliance, and they conducted local elections for local AIM leaders. Many of the people that were elected for the chairmanships of the local chapters were people who would never be good leaders. They were drunken people, uneducated people, not respectful, and did not believe in working within the system. I didn't think they should be elected. This is what started the friction between AIM and the American Indian Council and myself.

AIM started badgering me personally and the American Indian Council as a corporation. The American Indian Council was establishing programs and serving Indian people. The local Indian leaders that AIM elected were jealous of the American Indian Council. They saw the council working within the system, so they decided not to work with us. I don't know whether this was supported by the national leaders or not. But it obviously didn't stop us from continuing our work to bring in good programs and serve the people.

The council's success only caused more hatred and friction between AIM, myself, and the American Indian Council; there were some violent episodes, and I am very much against that. I think the pitting of one Indian against another by AIM in our local communities could have been stopped if the national Indian movement had had some type of control over their local leaders. I believe I have met many of the national

AIM leaders, and they were very intelligent people. But they seemed to forget how jealous Indian people can be of each other. I'm very glad I wasn't a local AIM leader, but I feel very sorry that the American Indian Movement didn't work out. It has completely vanished from our area now. During the 1970s some of the local Indian leaders of AIM got into a lot of trouble; they were convicted of killing people. If the national AIM had only set up some type of control over all local leaders, the national American Indian Movement would have been a success.

We leased the Indian Center building, and I think the AIM movement was jealous. They didn't want the city of Alliance renting the building to Mark Monroe for only one dollar a year. They'd go to a city council meeting and tell them lies about what we were doing. They'd degrade our council, which made me very unhappy—because I knew and our board knew and our community knew that we had good, productive programs that were helping Indian people. When AIM started attacking our programs and then saw that tactic didn't work, the next thing they did was to attack our building lease.

I asked the city council to sell the building to the American Indian Council, but there was a regulation that they could not sell any city property to another organization. So I asked them to sell it to me personally, and I would put it on the tax rolls, making the American Indian Council a tax-paying, productive organization. That night the AIM members here in Alliance also attended the meeting and opposed my request. They said they wanted the building for their own programs. AIM didn't have any programs, and everybody in Alliance knew it. The mayor, who had come to our center many times to view our programs and knew how successful they were, supported us. He told the AIM leader he'd give them a lot and the material to build their own center. He even offered to have the material hauled to the lot and have the town carpenters build the center. The AIM people re-

jected the offer. They wanted our building. The offer was
open for one week, but AIM didn't accept it. This made the
city council mad.

Then a week later, the American Indian Center building went up for sale, and AIM could have purchased it, but
didn't. The building was sitting on city property next to a
park; the city council wanted whoever purchased the building
to move it to a different location, with a sanitary system,
sewer system, and whatever was needed to bring the building
up to code. Two years earlier I had purchased two lots far-
ther up the road that were perfect for the center. That night I
went to the city council and bid twenty-five dollars for the
building. There were no other bids. That was April 1977. I
had thirty days to move the center to our new location. So I
hired a contractor, although I only had $2,000 or $3,000 in
the bank at that time. The contractor went on top of the hill
where the center is now and poured the cement. He moved
the building up to the new location. For about three months,
we had to shut down our programs, but the much nicer location was worth it. When the building was set back on the
ground, I renovated the building with my own private money.
It cost $27,000 to put the building on the ground. This in-
cluded the sewer system, rewiring, and renovating the building. Emma and I paid these bills as they came in. I don't
know how we did it, but when the building was completed, it
was paid for.

AIM couldn't figure out where to attack us. The books
for the American Indian Council's programs were in order,
and everything was well run. They couldn't take the the
building so nothing much came out of all the arguments and
complaints from AIM and some of our local Indian people
who weren't part of the movement. Things settled down a little bit with the building at a different location. After we got
moved and settled in, the programs ran well. My family and I
had an apartment at the back of the building. One Sunday
night about seven o'clock—I think it was in April 1978,
shortly after we had moved in—one of our AIM leaders

named Bob Yellow Bird and five or six of his henchmen walked into the building without knocking. I was sitting in my living room. Bob Yellow Bird looked in and said, "Monroe, I want to see you outside." So I walked out. My son Daryl, who was probably twenty-two or twenty-three years old at that time and a pretty good-sized man, was also there, along with my grandson Mark, my daughter Hope, who was very young, and my wife. As I walked into the hallway, Bob Yellow Bird hit me. I doubled over and felt a pistol in my stomach. I thought he was going to kill me. I managed to push him down the hallway, where the other five men and Bob Yellow Bird's wife were standing. I ran into the bedroom where I keep pistols, but I remembered that my son Terry and I hadn't loaded them back up after cleaning them. By the time I got one and started loading it, Yellow Bird had come into our living quarters and put his pistol to Emma's head and asked her where I was. He thought I was running away from him. He also pointed the pistol at the children and Daryl. Each one of them thought that they were going to be shot.

When Yellow Bird saw me coming with my gun, he ran away. I had every intention of killing this man because he came to kill us. But they all jumped in their car and started to take off. I shot all six bullets into their car as they drove away.

When the police did not respond to our call, I called the sheriff's department. As we were giving our stories to the sheriff, the AIM people regrouped and came by again, shooting at our center while the sheriff was there. By this time my two boys, Daryl and Terry, had gone up on the roof and were firing their rifles back at them. The two carloads of AIM people were riding around our center shooting at us with rifles, handguns, and shotguns. The sheriff ran out and started chasing them in his car, but while he was chasing one car, the other one full of AIM people attacked me and my family. We had a war going on here, and it lasted until one o'clock in the morning. Even now, I don't know how anybody avoided getting killed. The next day the police found approximately fifty bullet holes in the building.

Later, Bob Yellow Bird was caught but was never convicted. The defense lawyer asked for a change of venue to Scottsbluff. My whole family attended and testified. But, Bob Yellow Bird got up holding a peace pipe and said that when an Indian holds a peace pipe, he cannot lie. He completely fooled the white jury, and Yellow Bird convinced them he was innocent. He did admit to hitting me. The judge gave him a choice of either serving thirty days in jail or attending an alcohol treatment center. Yellow Bird ended up doing neither; he went to Pine Ridge Reservation, South Dakota, and refused to come back. None of the others with him were sentenced further.

AIM never did arouse much cultural awareness among the Indians. A lot of people were ashamed to be members of that organization. I am glad I didn't become an AIM leader. To me, they were just a bunch of hoodlums. They came to Alliance, threatened people, and threw rocks through their windows. When they left, it was very bad for us who were residents of this town. There had been all this racism before, and now we got the white backlash.

A letter from Ken Lincoln had appeared in the "Rumblings" column in the Alliance *Times Herald* on April 8, 1975, responding to an editorial in the paper that had severely criticized the violence caused in our town by the American Indian Movement (AIM). Ken didn't excuse their conduct, but he spoke eloquently for a binding up of the wounds. He proposed that Alliance should make a new beginning. There should be an Indian medical staff of one doctor and a team of nurses, Indian teachers in public schools, and schoolwide instruction on American Indian heritage and culture. Our low-grade housing should be improved with better roads, utilities, and the kind of services enjoyed by the rest of Alliance. He pointed out that we needed to have Indian public servants and city officials and Indian people in local businesses working for a fair share of the community's wealth. All of this could be accomplished, Ken pointed out, with the active support of the non-Indian people. I admired Ken for what he said, but I knew that it would be a long time before we had many of these things in Alliance.

In spite of all the adversity, we all managed to continue our programs. We have been able to work freely and honestly, providing these programs which are much needed and administering them successfully. We are still the only active center in western Nebraska providing meals and health and housing services. There are probably six or seven other towns that have large Indian communities, but they are unable to get programs like ours started because of the distrust, hatred, and jealousy within the Indian communities themselves. Fortunately, in Alliance we've been able to work together and do everything that it takes to run a good organization. I think that's the reason why we're still in business today.

About two weeks ago a man from Scottsbluff came to our Indian center and asked me if I would go to Scottsbluff and develop these kinds of programs for the Indian people there. I'm sure they have some potential Indian leaders, but no one has ever done anything to get any of these programs started. So I told this man that if he had a meeting in Scottsbluff, got the Indian people together, and made sure that these programs were the kinds of things that they wanted, and they wanted me as their administrator, I'd go and set a program up for them basically the same as ours.

I don't know what is going to happen now, but I think what the American Indian Council has been able to prove is that if the people in an Indian community want a program and they work hard enough to get it, they will get one. I've been able to create programs and lead our Indian people in the Alliance community and in other adjoining communities. We've provided this kind of image for the rest of the Indian people. Now it's up to them to do it. Every program we have here in Alliance is a needed program. There is no waste.

C·H·A·P·T·E·R XII

LOVED ONES
Losses and Recoveries

The year 1978 was a turning point for my family. A period of terrible sadness started with the death of my oldest son, Terry. He had Mother's Day dinner with us that May 14, 1978, and left home about six-thirty in the evening, riding the motorcycle he loved so much down the alley. Approximately twenty-five minutes later, the telephone rang, and the doctor who had treated him was calling to tell me that Terry had passed away. I was so shocked, I couldn't believe it, and I kept asking the doctor, "Are you sure this is my son Terry?" He said, "Yes, Terry was in a motorcycle accident, and he died here at the hospital." Emma, our daughters Connie and Hope, and the rest of the family were all sitting around the kitchen table. I think I turned around and told Emma that Terry had died. I may have fainted or something for a few minutes.

My wife wanted me to go to the hospital with her to identify Terry and see him, but I just couldn't do it. So Connie, Emma, and Hope went without me. While they were gone, I must have got some composure back because I had been walking around the center crying and hollering. I remember that very well. At this point I just couldn't control myself. Emma, who has always been the strongest of our family, did go to the hospital, but when they brought her back, she fainted and was carried into the house.

I could not accept the fact that I had lost my oldest son, who I loved with all my heart and soul. The next morning Emma and I were sitting around the table when she told me that Terry had always said that his dad was the kind of man who could handle things. He was a take-charge guy. I

knew that I had to accept Terry's death. That afternoon
Emma and the girls went to view Terry's body at the mortuary, but I didn't want to go yet. However, Emma told me I
had to. So later that afternoon I went to the mortuary and
viewed my boy's body. Even though I knew that somehow or
another God must have prepared me for this type of thing, I
just didn't react right. I accepted it and tried to be as brave as
possible, but there were times when I didn't think I could
hold up.

My oldest son was a tall, good-looking boy who had
accepted the Indian way. He was very proud of his heritage
and wore his hair in long braids. At one point after his death,
I was told that he was asking one of our holy men to explain
to him what life was about in the Indian way. He was probably planning on learning the Indian medicine part of it to
help people. He died on the fourteenth, and we buried him
on his twenty-fourth birthday. As days went by, I regained
my strength and ability to accept what had happened. Shortly
after Terry died, Emma wanted to bury the damn motorcycle
on our Indian Center property, but I said no. So I sold it for
$400, as we needed the money. Emma had a much harder
time. For one entire year she cut her hair close to the scalp
and wore black clothes in memory of our son.

When Emma had found out in 1956 that she had sugar
diabetes, she immediately started a diet, cooked the right
food, and the whole family agreed to eat the same way she
did. It seemed like we were eating better when Emma had her
sugar diabetes than prior to that. I learned how to administer
her insulin shots and even though she had this disease, she
seemed to be very normal. When we lost our son, she quit
taking care of herself. It was as though she just didn't want
to live anymore or accept life without him. I noticed right
away that she was not the same person and that she had just
given up.

Before Terry died, he was living with a Swedish girl
named Judy. In October of 1978 she had twins—a little boy

we named Terry and a little girl, Shannon. The twins were
born prematurely in Pine Ridge, but they were taken to Denver, Colorado, for better care. Somehow during this time
Judy went there and gave the twins to the Social Service Department. Emma had been up there to see the babies two or
three times with Connie. They fell in love with them, and
when they found out what Judy had done, they went right to
Denver.

Fortunately, at that time, the Indian Child Welfare Act
had come into being; it required that Indian children go only
into Indian foster homes or to their grandparents. So I called
an attorney in Omaha who was a very good friend, and he
called a judge. Emma talked to the judge herself and told him
that she wanted the children. So the twins, Terry and Shannon, were given to her.

I think it was January 1, 1979, that Emma and Connie
brought them home, and Emma and I legally adopted them
that year. Connie said she would keep Shannon, and Emma
and I said we would keep Terry. The first time Terry came
home, Emma placed him in the middle of our bed, and that's
where he stayed. Emma was too ill at that time to change his
diaper or get his bottle, so I took over those chores for her.
In the middle of the night I'd get up with him. Terry became
my son. He loved Emma very much and called her Unci,
which is "grandmother" in Indian, and he called me Dad. He
called my youngest daughter, Hope, Mom. It was very con-
fusing to some people who came to our house. My daughter
Connie still has Shannon. I think everything worked out for
the best. The main thing is, we got the children back.

In the middle part of 1979 Emma became very ill. We
took her to Pine Ridge Hospital, where they found that her
kidneys were real bad. In October she was sent to Min-
neapolis, Minnesota, to have a shunt put in her arm so that
she could have dialysis treatment. During this time Emma lost
so much weight and so much of her pride and her desire to
live that we all noticed it. In December Emma began going to

Scottsbluff, about sixty miles away, for dialysis treatment. Connie, Kandi, or I would drive her there three times a week.

All this time Emma had complications and her health deteriorated. Once she stepped on a small piece of glass; she didn't feel it because the diabetes had numbed her feet, and the doctors didn't see it. Gangrene set in, but she wouldn't let them cut her foot off. So the doctors did the next best thing; they cut the sole and toes off her right foot. She suffered from that up until the time she died. Even though she didn't mind too much what the doctors did to her foot, she would never show it to me, as she figured I wouldn't like it. She was more concerned about my feelings than hers. Going to Scottsbluff three times a week really undermined her health and was awfully hard on all of us.

On the Friday before Mother's Day in May 1981, I was out working on my lawn at the center and had a terrible headache and dizzy spells. That Sunday we had a nice Mother's Day party, but the next day I had a stroke. My daughter Kandi drove me to Scottsbluff. On the way up there a patrol car stopped us, as we were doing fifty-six miles an hour. Kandi was on probation for reckless driving, and her license had been revoked, so she was arrested and taken to the Bridgeport county jail. I told the patrolman that she was taking me to the hospital because I was very sick. He didn't seem to care, and I drove the rest of the way into Scottsbluff by myself.

When I arrived there, I was so disoriented and so weak that I couldn't even walk. I managed to get the car parked somehow and to get into the hospital. I just leaned up against the wall and stood there because I was getting dizzy and very weak. The social worker who had worked with Emma quite a bit came over and asked what was wrong; I told her, and she immediately took me to a doctor. The doctor, a neurosurgeon, did not want to deal with me at that time. I don't know if it was because I was an Indian or because he had too many patients to see. So I was taken to an eye doctor, who examined me and said, "Well, you had a stroke. Your right peripheral vision is completely gone." That's when he called in the neurosurgeon and told him that he had better work with me or I would die just like the guy he refused to work with the day before. At this point I was becoming very frightened. In the hallway I had told the social worker that my son Daryl lived in Scottsbluff. After she got me to the doctor, she called Daryl. He was very concerned and stayed with me.

The doctor said I had had a stroke on Friday and two more strokes on Sunday. I stayed in the hospital for one week. When I was admitted, the nurses wouldn't pay any attention to me. Nobody would get me a glass of water; they just put me up on a bed, where I stayed. The two other men in the same room were given water and were treated; people gave them whatever they wanted. For some reason the nurses wouldn't even look at me. So when the neurosurgeon came in to see me, I said to him, "Doctor, I want to talk to you someplace alone." I was very weak at this point. He took me to a private room somewhere down the hallway. I leaned over him and said, "Doctor, who in the hell do you think you are? First of all, you don't want to work with me and second, you put me in a room where the nurses ignore me. You're no good as a doctor. I believe you think you're God, and that you can pick out the people whom you want to work with."

My intention really was to reach over and hit him in the face, because I thought he was a belligerent, racist, arrogant type of person. I didn't expect what happened next. He asked me if they were really treating me that badly, and I said they were. He sat there and thought for a while; then he apologized and thanked me for telling him. He escorted me back to my room, and within a very few minutes the nurses were treating me very kindly and going out of their way to do things for me. The next morning I began taking all kinds of tests and x-rays. The doctor came in with a wheelchair and pushed me to the lab that day. When we arrived back at my room, I heard the other two men and one of the nurses say that they had never seen him treat one of his patients that way.

I used to go back to that doctor for checkups, and he became a very good, personal friend of mine until he moved away several years later.

When I was released from the hospital, Emma came to get me after her dialysis treatment, and we came home together. After we got back, from May 1981 on, I could see how much Emma was deteriorating. Her health was very bad, and dialysis didn't seem to be doing her any good. In my mind I would say to her, "Emma, please stay alive until I can get well." I didn't want both of us to leave our children at the same time or so close together. Emma kind of sensed this and gave me a little time to recuperate. I knew that I was going to lose my wife, but I didn't know when.

After I was back from the hospital for maybe a week, Loretta Whirlwind Horse, who is Emma's sister-in-law, arranged a *lowanpi* (sing) with Dawson No Horse, the Pine Ridge medicine man, at Wakpamni Lake in South Dakota, to treat me. So Emma, my brother-in-law George, my sister-in-law Lulu, and Emma's sister Dorothy drove me approximately one hundred miles to this place where the "sing" was to take place. Emma was terminally ill at this time, and I knew she probably didn't have enough strength to go, but she wanted to anyway. George, who is kind of a clown, always joking and raising heck, was telling me all the way down there what they were going to do to me and what was going to happen. All I hoped for was that I had enough courage to go through with it. Especially with Emma there; I didn't want her knowing that I fainted or died during the "sing."

A *lowanpi* is done in complete darkness. The medicine man, Dawson No Horse, was tied up with ropes and then wrapped in a star quilt. He couldn't see anything, and I couldn't either. He had told me at the beginning of the cere-

mony that an eagle would come. Well, when he began singing, sure enough the eagle did come. I felt its wings brushing
against my face. It was the eeriest feeling. I had never been a
patient of a medicine man before, so I was very scared. Fortunately, Emma was there sitting next to me.

It was such a beautiful ceremony. I think the medication that the doctor gave me and this *lowanpi* kind of
brought me back. (But, of course, even today I still don't
have my right peripheral vision.) It made me so happy that
all these people in our family thought so much of me to go to
all that trouble on my behalf. It was such a beautiful feeling
to know that people cared for me. I think this feeling of happiness and caring probably made me better.

That summer Emma began to deteriorate more. I always hoped that she would not die or leave us, because I
wasn't strong enough to accept her death or be able to take
care of my children with the shape I was in. Maybe Emma
sensed this somehow and prolonged her death until January
24, 1982. I don't know, but things worked out that way. She
was a person who could really sense what you were feeling.
So I believe Emma really did hold on to her life a little while
longer.

The last time Emma went to the hospital in Scottsbluff
where they had the dialysis unit, she had been going downhill
fast for about eight months. She left on a Thursday morning
to have her foot operated on again. Before she left, she
peeked in on Terry and me as we were lying in bed about
five-thirty in the morning. I didn't think too much of it at the
time. Connie was taking her up there. Sometime Friday afternoon Emma called me from Scottsbluff Hospital and said
that her blood pressure had dropped clear to zero. She didn't
have any blood pressure. I had gone through this so many
times before with her that I didn't take it as anything special.
Now I think it was Emma's way of telling me to come up
there right away this time. She didn't say that, of course, be-

cause I was taking care of Terry, who was only about three
years old. To this day, I regret not going up there as soon as
Emma called.

All day Saturday I was thinking about her. On Sunday
I bussed elderly Presbyterian people to church, so right after
twelve o'clock I got into the car and went up to see her. I remember that the wind was so strong that the car could barely
move, but I got up there. She was in her room, and she
looked so beautiful, vibrant, and healthy sitting and smil-
ing—just like the girl I met way back in 1946. I really
thought that. The doctor told Emma that she could come
back home on Wednesday. So we were sitting there just talking normally, and I was telling her that I would be up there
Wednesday to get her. Emma asked for a candy bar, so I
went down to get her one, and a couple of malts for myself. I
love chocolate malts. Later, she was sitting there eating her
candy and I was sitting right next to her, only a couple of
inches away, talking and watching the Super Bowl. All of a
sudden a nurse came in, looked at Emma, and said, "Emma,
what is the matter with you?" It couldn't have been more
than thirty to forty-five seconds from the last time I heard her
talk and I had spoken to her. Right away they called the code
blue for the hospital, and all the technicians came with the
respirator and machinery to try to revive her. I waited and
waited outside in the hall. They must have administered
emergency aid to Emma for an hour. Finally, the doctor came
out and told me that she had died. I absolutely couldn't believe him. I was so shocked. I had been sitting so close to
Emma that I could feel her. She never reached over to
squeeze my hand or gasped hard. I didn't hear anything. She
just quietly died.

My son Daryl and my nephew Percy, who also lived
there in Scottsbluff, came over to where I was sitting. A
Catholic priest was talking to me, but I don't remember what
he said. I felt so helpless. Emma didn't want to scare or
shock anybody. If she had problems, she worked them out

herself. That afternoon when I went to see her, she went into the bathroom, combed her hair real pretty, and put on a little lipstick. Nobody in the world would ever have guessed that she was going to die, but I think she knew. She knew what a big coward I am and that I couldn't stand to know what was going to happen, so she did not reach out to me and say, "Good-bye" or anything.

After Emma's death and her funeral, I went to talk to her doctor. I could not accept Emma's death, so I wanted to know how it happened. The doctors told me that her arteries had all clogged up and that her heart had been in bad shape. She had been this way for quite a while, he explained, but she had never told me about it. After the doctor explained all these things to me, I still could not accept Emma's death. I know now there was absolutely nothing I could have done to prevent it. That was very hard for me to accept. Emma died like the kind of person she was. It was her way of life and her way of dying—I think it was a beautiful way to go. She wasn't afraid; she had been a good woman all her life and very religious, and she died that way.

We had Emma's wake in our center, and when her body was lying there, she was still the most beautiful woman I had ever seen. I was so shocked that I didn't even put on her wedding rings and bury her with them. Our daughters, Hope, Kandi, and Connie, had ordered a corsage. They gave it to me and asked me to put it on Emma. As I was pinning it on her breast, it finally hit me that Emma was leaving me forever. Right then and there I broke down, and cried and cried. Too late. We buried my wife January 27. Emma was one in a million. I still feel that way about her, and I always will. I loved her with my whole heart and soul.

Looking back, I think my little grandson Terry must have known his grandmother was gone for good. He loved her very much. Terry and I were home alone on the Thursday night after she left for the hospital. It was very cold and blizzarding that night; must have been twenty degrees below zero. I was carrying Terry around the apartment, and he looked out of the bedroom window. Even though Terry still was only three, he had a premonition that something terrible was going to happen. He looked out and said "Unci, Unci." He started crying. I felt that Terry saw his grandmother, Emma, in the window. It was unbelievable, but I somehow felt that he sensed his grandmother was going to die, because they were very close. Emma loved Terry with all her heart, and she didn't want to leave him.

Some of these things are a wonderment. I'm still trying to figure out how they all happened and how much Emma thought of us. Still, it gives me a kind of strange feeling when I talk about it. About the first or second night after her burial, Terry saw his grandmother again. We were lying in bed, and all of a sudden he started calling "Unci." I knew that Emma had come back and was lying where she always did, with Terry in the middle between us. She was there that night. So I said, "Emma, leave Terry alone because you're scaring him and he is crying." Pretty soon, Terry quieted down again. I knew Emma had come back and was still with us. I could feel it so clearly, and so could Terry.

When I was lying there in bed at night with Terry beside me, I would feel so lonesome that I could have died. If it hadn't been for my little grandson, I probably would have. I would pray every night, and somehow I could sense when Emma was with us. Terry would get fidgety and move around. I sensed Emma's presence with us. When I hear of people being scared of ghosts, I can say I never felt that way. I would lie in the same bed that Emma and I had shared for years and years and would never be scared. I always had the feeling that she was with us, taking care of us.

The strangest thing happened one night about two weeks after we buried her. As I lay there praying and missing her so much, I felt Emma was so close to me that I could just reach out and touch her. I could feel her face right next to mine. She bent over and kissed me right on my lips. That kiss was so warm and so real that it was like she was right there. She left us for good after that. It was one of the most beautiful moments in my life, and one I'll always remember.

I felt so calm, so happy knowing that my wife was still somewhere watching over us. Emma had a habit of popping her knuckles when she'd get nervous. Well, I've lain awake at nights and heard her knuckles pop and have known somehow that Emma was still with me. I live in a large building with a lot of rooms, and before we moved in the place, people said that it was one of the spookiest places in town. I never have been scared or afraid living here.

With the deaths of Terry and Emma, I almost began drinking again, but something within me wouldn't let me, because I knew I had the rest of my family to take care of. Even though my oldest daughter, Connie, was married, and my son Daryl, too, I still had Hope and Terry, whom I'm raising now. I had to be sober to take care of them.

My daughter Kandi, who had spent a lot of time with her Mom, also had sugar diabetes and suffered with it ever since she was seven or eight years old. She also had a shunt put in her arm so she could go on dialysis, which she did shortly after her mother died. Each one of our family members would drive Kandi to Scottsbluff to the hospital and make the 110-mile round trip every Monday, Wednesday, and Friday. I'm very thankful that I've got my daughter Connie and my daughter Hope, who helped me. One day I took Kandi to the dialysis unit, where she went into a coma. She was supposed to die the very same day, but I stayed with her for the two weeks she remained in the coma. I called my family and everybody came, and most of us stayed with her until her death, on May 31, 1984. These were very, very sad times for my entire family.

I would sit back and thank God and my family that I was able to maintain my sobriety through all of this grief and loneliness. It's a wonder that I didn't become a self-pitying alcoholic again. However, I think Emma had a lot to do with preparing me, not only for the gift of sobriety but also for the gift of accepting the deaths in our family. I think many other people did also—people such as my mother-in-law, Jenny Lone Wolf, and Mr. Chips, the medicine man who worked with me. I still find it hard living without Emma, even after these twelve years. Whenever I have a problem or something goes wrong in my life, I'll say to myself, "Where's Emma?" Then I'll remember she's no longer here to help me. God, it gives a man the emptiest feeling.

My grandson Terry has kept me going. We still live in the apartment in the center building. He is now fifteen years old and in the eighth grade. He serves on the student council and is a star athlete. He loves football. Terry is an exceptional boy, and I am very proud of him.

My son Daryl recently became a deputy sheriff. He graduated from the police academy in Grand Island, Nebraska. We all went up to the ceremony. I'm proud of him and that he now has become a law officer in the United States. He and his wife, Tammy, have four children.

My daughter Hope has been hired as our school counselor for Indian students here in Alliance. She was hired by the Title V program through advertising in the local newspaper. I think that's a very democratic way. Twenty people applied for the job, but Hope was best qualified. Now I'm a member of the Title V board of directors, so when we were voting to hire Hope, I abstained and left the room. It was the Indian parents who hired her, and they did this on their own. In the one year since she's been working, Hope has done a very good job. About a week ago she and several children came to me and asked if they could start a new Boy Scout troop. Would I be their scoutmaster? They wanted me to also help start a dance organization. I sure was pleased. I think what I had done some years ago is coming back through Hope's teaching. The children remembered what happened. Hopefully, the parents will be more motivated than they were when our Boy Scout troop disbanded years ago. There was just no follow-up at that time, and nobody willing to take over as scoutmaster when I couldn't continue. Hope plans on starting Boy Scouts and a dance troop soon. I'm glad I'm still here to help. Hope married Keith Baker after she graduated from high school, and they have a son.

Connie, my oldest daughter, has become our medicine woman, following in the footsteps of her grandmother, Jenny Lone Wolf. She apprenticed herself to Joe Eagle Elk, the medicine man who lived at St. Francis, South Dakota, on the Rosebud Indian Reservation before he died. Connie went through the traditional ceremonies of fasting, the sweat lodge, vision quest, and sun dance. She has been able to help a number of people. I believe Indian medicine is very strong. Some of the things that Connie has done for people are hard to explain. I think if a person went to her, she could heal them mentally and physically, but I don't know how she does it. Connie and her husband, Gary Stairs, have six children, including Kandi's son, whom they adopted when his mother died.

Someone recently asked how I felt about intermarriage. Well, I had never thought much about it. Every one of my children is now married to a white person, and I love my sons-in-law and my daughter-in-law very much. We always kid whenever we have a family reunion and somebody takes a picture of us. I feel like a fly sitting in a bowl of milk because I really show up. I'm so dark skinned. We all laugh and get a big kick out of it. My children all married good people, and they get along real good. That makes me happy. I really don't know whether I'm for or against intermarriage, but I think when people meet at school or social events, it's bound to happen.

Shortly after Emma died, I received a letter and a check for our American Indian Council from Mrs. Carolyn Reyer. I didn't know Lynn (as we call her) at that time, but over the past twelve years she has become a close personal friend of mine. My daughters adopted her as their mother after Emma

died, and they love her very much. Lynn has been the most
helpful and caring person I've ever known. She's done so
much for me, my family, and for the Indians in Alliance.
When I decided I'd like to try writing a book, I asked her to
help me with it and have provided her with all the tapes, letters, photographs, and articles on which this story of my life
is based.

Thinking back over past events in my life, so I could
talk about them in this book, I've wondered why it was so
hard for me to talk about my Korean war experiences. I felt
that anyone who had not been there couldn't understand the
terrible fear I felt and the horrible things witnessed. They are
just indescribable. Now I'm comfortable talking to my son-in-
law Gary, who was in combat in Vietnam. I can understand
what Gary's been through, and he can understand what happened to me. We've both been in combat and come back, but
I'm finding out now that people really don't care whether
you served in the war or not. They really don't give a damn
anymore about Korea or Vietnam.

Being in the Army was a positive experience for me in
some ways and for other Indians, also. Indians have always
had a proud heritage of serving their country. I read in the
Lakota *Times* that 85 percent of Native Americans who went
into the services enlisted. They did not wait to be drafted. Be-
sides wanting to serve, there were other reasons. There were
no jobs here in Alliance for American Indians. We could not
attend regular school, so there was not much else left to do
except to enlist. When I was in the Army, there was preju-
dice, and there still is. I held my head high around the officers and enlisted men. Many of them respected me. I think
being in the Army helped me to learn respect, discipline, and
how to work and be neat. To this day I don't feel good unless I have on a pressed shirt, a clean pair of pants, and
shined shoes.

There was a dark side to my war experiences in Korea,
however. I came back scarred not only physically but emo-

tionally and mentally as well. It has taken me a long, long time to say that my war experience made a coward out of me. I've always wondered if that emotional scarring didn't cause me to turn to alcohol. I know that there were a lot of young soldiers like me who went into combat and came back the same way. Over the years since I sobered up, I've learned to speak out on a number of Indian issues; I do a lot of things here in Alliance and Nebraska as an Indian advocate. But, you see, I'm still having a heck of a time with this thinking that I'm a coward. I don't think I'll ever get over it.

The American Indian Council, Inc., has become a strong institution. We have a state charter and tax-deductible status from the U.S. government, so we have to operate under the rules for a county-seat organization. When we hold elections, we put up notices on our center walls and in our local newspaper. About twenty-five to thirty people normally show up; they elect our officers and the board of directors by a show of hands or by ballot. The council is administered and governed entirely by Indian people, so we don't have any non-Indians serving. The exception has been my son-in-law Gary, who's been an Indian all his life. I've never questioned it. He was elected by our people, and that's all our by-laws call for.

We have a very good relationship with most of the civic, county, and church organizations. The United Way used to support us. However, two very prejudiced people got on their board, and they persuaded the others to stop funding us. Nothing would change their minds. The majority of people in Alliance were very upset over the stance the United Way took. It was so obvious that it was a problem of racism.

Now we are getting support for our programs from such organizations as Ronald MacDonald Charities; MAZON-A Jewish Response to Hunger; the First Presbyterian Church and the First Baptist Church in Alliance; the Inner Church Ministries in Lincoln, Nebraska; the counties of Box Butte, Sheridan, and Scottsbluff; the Box Butte Presbytery, which includes all the Presbyterian churches in north-western Nebraska; and many individuals around the state.

I am proud that I am an Indian and a member of the Oglala Sioux tribe. I believe in our cultural heritage, but I also know that if Indians are going to survive in America, they have to change their ways and learn to live in both the Indian and white worlds.

I am also proud that I live off the reservation, even though conditions here have been so terrible that I've some-times compared Alliance to Nazi Germany during World War II. Sometimes I think the only difference is they didn't line us up and kill us. I feel proud that I've been able to endure those conditions and still be a human being—a proud, sober, and productive one. In my mind I think, God, those guys living on the reservation have got it made. They've got free homes, free hospitalization, free schools and commodities, all from the U.S. government as part of its treaty responsibility. In Alliance we have to struggle for everything we get. There are no free government benefits for us. However, hard as it is, I am proud that I don't have to live that way, because I think I'm better off than they are.

I'm also very proud that I have had so many people like my wife, Emma; my family; Ken Lincoln; Lynn Reyer; Dawson No Horse, the medicine man who helped me; Dr. Durken; and others at Fort Meade and Hot Springs, South Dakota, who believed in me. Even though some things didn't work out, at least these people cared and have tried. I owe my life and everything I've become to them.

Even though conditions for Indians have become better in Alliance during the last decade or so, they still are not good. Discrimination is just more subtle. Sometimes I sit down and try to figure out why an Indian is so different from a white man; it seems that neither side ever tries to find out what we can do about our differences. Even though racism still exists, I see some very positive things coming out of our

Indian population as they are overcoming their fear of the white majority and becoming good citizens.

At this time in my life I feel proud about the programs I've started, which are helping a lot of people. What I think now is that anybody—an Indian, a black, a Mexican-American, a low-income white person—can decide what he or she wants to do with his or her life and do it. An alcoholic can decide to stay sober. Anyone can become the person who runs for city council or for the job of county commissioner. Even in a town where racism exists, a person can overcome it. This is the type of person I've become. I'm a man who has wanted to help the Indian people, and I've set about designing programs that will make it happen. Though people say I'm a leader, I say I'm just an *ikcè wicàsà*—"a common man"—who's trying to make a living and provide for his family.

A·F·T·E·R·W·O·R·D

Some years ago in our hometown my brother Mark Monroe and I talked outside the American Indian Center. As Lakota and Caucasian men in Alliance, we embodied peoples at war across the Buckskin Curtain for centuries. Indians and whites have been tragically estranged in northwest Nebraska: Wounded Knee directly north, pioneer ruts to the south. This was exclusive Sioux territory until the 1880s, then little more than a westering land grab.

That August afternoon, rain clouds bellied over the rolling green sandhills. The expanse of shortgrass and thick sky caught us like a gust of prairie wind.

"Sometimes I look out there," Mark said under his breath, "and see Indians on ponies, just like it used to be, with herds of buffalo. Damn, it's changed."

A man has the need to dream, to measure the distance from past to present, to recall his time and witness changes. As tape recorded for Carolyn Reyer, Mark's story is the self-narrated witness of a Sioux warrior born out of the old ways into the hardpan modern world. "It's tough," Mark says, "to be an Indian in white America." Mark's dreams of common dignity carry the legends of Crazy Horse and Red Cloud into the contemporary history of Mahatma Gandhi, John Kennedy, and Martin Luther King, Jr. His story charts a powerful change in Western ethnic dialogue where *Native* Americans now speak for themselves as peacemakers. The country is turning to listen. Recognition for such figures as Vine Deloria, Jr. (Lakota), Louise Erdrich (Chippewa), N. Scott Momaday (Kiowa), and Leslie Silko (Laguna Pueblo) traces back to local origins in Indian country.

Mark was born in the heart of Sioux country, Buzzard Basin, South Dakota, 1930, and named Stone Arrow after his maternal grandfather. As a child he lived in a one-room log cabin on the Rosebud Reservation during the Depression. When his paternal grandfather, John Long Time Sleep, toured Europe with the Buffalo Bill Wild West Show, he took the name Monroe. The family renamed themselves Monroe and moved off-reservation to a log cabin in Wood, South Dakota, where Mark's four extended "grandfathers" camped in tents around the family *tiospaye*. Grampa Leo hunted for his meat and boiled live turtle stew in a corrugated tub, and an extended aunt cooked cow or horse hooves as a delicacy.

In 1941 the Monroes relocated to Alliance, Nebraska, where the father, Bill, found work during the war: "Everything changed for us there," Mark recalls. "Many times I was to look back on those days in Wood and remember how good our life had been."

In the spring of 1969 Mark ran for police magistrate in Alliance, a century after the 1868 Red Cloud Treaty promised the Sioux northwest Nebraska and the Dakotas in perpetuity. No Indian had ever filed for public office in our hometown. Almost none was registered to vote. So, needing three hundred signatures on his petition, Mark led five inmates at a time (the indentured garbage crew) from the city jail to the county courthouse, and ninety Sioux Indians were soon enrolled in Box Butte County. Stanley Standing Soldier gave his address as the city jail.

From bars to ladies' clubs, churches to the jail, Mark took a newfound candor and courage to the people. He spoke before an Elks Club symposium and stood on a chair to address working men at King's Korner Bar. He drafted an Indian bill of rights for the town: "All we wanted to do was to be heard, and to be respected." There were crank calls and public fights, rotten eggs and sidewalk scrawls, but something more than this—from both sides people of good heart crossed ethnic lines to show support, to offer services, to confront injustice and suffering. A lawyer tutored Mark, a reporter listened, a welfare director bought him respectable clothes, a plumber paid for a radio editorial. A century of corrosive racism came under local reexamination. Men and women began taking a second look at their frontier blood wars.

Here Mark and I became allies, soon adopted brothers, and I saw my hometown through Native American eyes, as documented in my book *The Good Red Road*. I was raised on redneck prejudices toward Indians. My father regarded them as uneducable, unemployable, unfit. Far too many townspeople ratified the bias. But, as children, we fished, swam, played ball, and ran together near a stream called Indian Creek; the natural world did not divide us racially.

Mark worked as a local baker's apprentice, when I would buy a ten-cent hot loaf of bread, on my way home from the pool hall after midnight. Younger members of his family went to public school beside me. By age twelve or thirteen, they started drinking, fighting with my white friends, turning to petty crime and prostitution, and dropping out of school. One of my Indian schoolmates broke into a liquor store and stole as much whiskey as he could carry, leaving the cash register untouched. He went to reform school, then prison.

I left my hometown for college in the early 1960s and returned as a family visitor to see the larger picture: a reservation to the north at Pine Ridge resembling a prisoner-of-war camp in an occupied military zone, my hometown an off-reservation Sioux ghetto for displaced refugees.

What causes, what effects help us to understand this situation of being "an Indian in white America"? The average family income at Pine Ridge was $1,500 a year ($125 a month) for families of eight to ten, and teenage suicide ran up to ten times the national average. The life expectancy of an American Indian in the 1950s was forty-four, and in my town probably ten years less. Education stopped at the fourth grade. Unemployment was epidemic, job skills all but nil. Mark

learned baking in the Army, and his brother took up beading
in the penitentiary. Alcoholism gutted up to 90 percent of the
Sioux population, including the Monroes. Malnutrition, diabetes, and tuberculosis ran rampant. In 1969 two teenage Indian boys hung themselves in our local jail. In this year Mark
made me his adopted brother.

I had some hard things to learn about human conditions
in my hometown. With Mark as my mentor, the last twenty
years have been a reeducation for me beyond any doctorate.

> The racial lines, which once were bitterly real, now
> serve nothing more than making out a living mosaic of
> human beings.
>   —Zitkala-Sa (Gertrude Bonin)
>   "Why I Am a Pagan," *Atlantic* (1902)

"Why, where, how did this racism start?" Mark asks,
remembering as a child when he could not go into the dime
store to buy a sandwich. "NO DOGS OR INDIANS," warned a
cardboard sign in the window. Because of their voluntary en-
listment in World War I, American Indians were granted dual
citizenship in 1924 but effectively denied the vote until the
1954 Civil Rights Act and federal threats of tribal termina-
tion. Ten years later Indian suffrage trickled into Alliance,
along with the right to buy alcohol.

During World War II Mark worked as a shoe-shine boy
for soldiers, as black MPs stood guard at the railroad under-
pass. Indians could not go uptown after 9:00 P.M. Later, en-
listing in the military liberated Mark from local apartheid: "It
was the only time that I felt accepted and liked as a human being." After bleeding in Korea for a country that declared war
on his own Sioux nation and returning with a Purple Heart to
a hero's welcome, Mark Monroe started a family with his
wife, Emma, that grew to five children. The *wicása wakán,* or
"man holy" Joe Chips, honored Mark with the warrior's
name *Mato Yamni,* meaning Three Bears. He was a warrior
struggling to come home.

Delayed stress, poverty, racism, and cultural despair turned Mark toward the anodyne of alcohol, and he was near fatally addicted. Stumbling down the suckhole of bootlegged booze, Mark struggled to rebuild a life from ground zero, his "last chance to live." Sun Dance warriors have long prayed, "Grandfather, pity me, I want to live," a prayer here translated into Mark's personal battle with the bottle: "Somewhere deep inside of me, something wanted to live again." His wife, Emma, still believed in "the man you were and will be."

This sense of native history, from personal life story to a people's witness, grounds American Indians in ancestral homelands today. It is another man's life in my hometown, my brother's story. His words tell the family core of tribal kinship, the roots of "we the people," a phrase Jefferson translated from the word *Iroquois.* "*Mitakuye oyasin,*" the Lakota say ceremonially, "all my relatives." To what extent we are all related poses a question of national, if not global imperative— neither heroes nor saints, but humankind nurtured interracially in Mother Earth. Warriors are battling to return peacefully as brothers among sisters. We all must gather in this extended kinship. Our future as interrelated human beings hangs in the balance.

"I didn't know where that country was or what we were fighting for in Korea. I killed a lot of people and saw the damage our guns did to some of the villages we raided. I've never wanted to talk about it very much." Mark's life story carries a legacy of terrible suffering met with courage, a warrior's narrative of Native American men, women, and children coming home through local wars for more than a century. Mark's wife, Emma bears five stillborn infants, victims of the diabetes that inexorably claims her life and her daughter Kandi's. Mark remembers digging the grave of one infant at Holy Rosary Mission in Pine Ridge; he had no money to buy a coffin or flowers, no way to bring the child's body back to Alliance.

From twelve pints of bad wine a day, picking through

trash barrels for empties, to facing the local power structures in Alliance, Mark fought to hold his head up. Beginning as a leader of the local American Indian Center, to becoming vice-president of the Nebraska Indian Commission, to becoming president of United Indians of Nebraska, Mark documents a story of recovery that reverses fatal statistics and dour stereotypes. In the last decade American Indian alcoholism has been cut by 50 percent and life expectancy has risen by more than ten years. Some fifty thousand Indian students are in college. Tuberculosis can be prevented, and diabetes can be successfully treated. And there is no excuse for starvation, still-birth, or endemic ethnic suffering in this richest of democratic nations. Times are changing. The cut of post-Holocaust humor salts Mark's gaze in looking back. "They knew that I was down and out," he says when alley winos offered their bottle, "but they never held my good part against me."

Mark's life is a story of heart and hard fact. It is told by a man "speaking the honest truth" as best he knows. No middleman writes for him or tells his story. Indeed, he "speaks" his own history directly and so is distinct from John Neihardt translating Nicholas Black Elk into holy man, or Richard Erdoes transcribing John (Fire) Lame Deer as intercultural healer, or Thomas Mails tracking Frank Fools Crow across South Dakota. The privacy of Mark's own home and reflection serve public witness to a people's narrative. If Luther Standing Bear collaborated with his wife on *My People the Sioux* and Charles Eastman self-consciously wrote *From the Deep Woods to Civilization,* in another voice Mark's own words record this life history as age-old talk among concerned kin, seeded within the oral tradition of tribal peoples. He is more interested in a daily, local dialogue with others than anyone I have known.

I can see Mark telling the story into a tape recorder. Leaning over a steelcase desk in the front room of the Indian Center, he's alone at night after a day filled with people—the hot lunch program for indigents (fifteen years now of feeding

some seventy thousand meals to more than two thousand people), telephone calls to local, state, and federal agencies, a
newspaper reporter inquiring about a job-training program,
an alcoholism counselor setting up an evening meeting, a
church representative checking on the hospital busing program
to Pine Ridge (more than ten thousand patients transported),
family members in and out all day long, his grandson Terry
home from school, drifters at the back door, outreach workers
at the front. Now by himself, Mark sips from a cup of coffee
long cold, lights a smoke, and taps on the metal desk with the
stiff fingers of his left hand. He remembers a life in astonish-
ing detail, shaping his story with imaginative accuracy.

Interracial conditions have changed for the better in Alliance, indeed in the country, though Indians still face a "hard
time and a long way to go." Lakota Indians no longer live in
army surplus tents south of the tracks in my hometown,
though none has yet to serve in public office, and all too few
finish high school. Cultural dignity and bicultural respect
mark the path into the future, along with steady jobs, sobriety, health care, decent housing, and access to professional
skills. South Alliance is now "integrated," Mark jokes, with
HUD housing for non-Indian railroaders, truckers, and up-
rooted farmers. Mark's children have married non-Indians,
and his grandchildren are positive fusions of cultures. Hope
counsels Indian students in the public schools, and Connie is
training as a native healer. Daryl is a county deputy sheriff.

The old-time vision of the red road is still a good one,
and Mark's voice joins the grandfather spirit Tunkáshila, as
dreamed by Nick Black Elk:

> When I looked behind me there were ghosts of people
> like a trailing fog as far as I could see—grandfathers of
> grandfathers and grandmothers of grandmothers with-
> out number. And over these a great Voice—the Voice
> that was the South—lived, and I could feel it silent.

And as we went the voice behind me said: *Behold a good nation walking in a sacred manner in a good land!*

Mark Monroe speaks one man's story of a native people coming home. I am honored to know this man as a brother; his story will long be remembered by our grandchildren.

Kenneth Lincoln